The Word of GOD and Pastoral Care

Howard W. Stone

Abingdon Press

Nashville

The Word of God and Pastoral Care

Copyright © 1988 by Abingdon Press

Library of Congress Cataloging-in-Publication Data

Stone, Howard W.
    Word of God and pastoral care / Howard W. Stone.
      p. cm.
    Includes index.
    ISBN 0-687-46133-2 (alk. paper)
    1. Pastoral theology. 2. Pastoral counseling. I. Title.
BV4011.S868   1988   88-6509
253—dc19   CIP

MANUFACTURED BY THE PARTHENON PRESS AT
NASHVILLE, TENNESSEE, UNITED STATES OF AMERICA

In memory of
Walter S. Stone
1910–1988

Acknowledgments

The "Introduction" appeared as "Religion as Taboo" in the *SPC Journal*, copyright © 1986 by the Lutheran Council in the USA. Used by permission.

A portion of chapter 1 originally appeared as "Pastoral Care in the 1980s" in *Religion in Life*, Autumn 1980, copyright © 1980 by Abingdon Press.

Chapter 2 originally appeared as "Theological Assessment in Pastoral Care" in *Dialog*, Winter 1982, copyright © 1982 by Dialog, Inc. John W. Schaub, who coauthored the article with Howard W. Stone, has granted permission for the present alterations and use. Every effort has been made to obtain permission from the publisher.

Chapter 3 originally appeared as "Word of God and Pastoral Care" in *Encounter*, Autumn 1983, copyright © 1983 by Christian Theological Seminary. Used by permission.

Chapter 4 originally appeared as "Left Brain, Right Brain" in *Theology Today*, October 1983, copyright © 1983 by Theology Today. Used by permission.

Chapter 5 appeared as "Spiritual Direction and Pastoral Counseling" in the *Journal of Pastoral Counseling*, Fall–Winter 1986, copyright © by Iona College Graduate Division of Pastoral Counseling. Used by permission.

Contents

Preface

Ever since seminary, when I first enrolled in a pastoral care class and wondered how those practical learnings could relate to what was taught in my theology classes, I have been intrigued and troubled by the problem of correlating theology with pastoral care and counseling. John Cobb's observation seems so apt:

The academic disciplines of theology and pastoral counseling have too long been at odds. In many seminary faculties their representatives have been suspicious of one another. Professors of theology have suspected that the beliefs that inform the teaching of counseling are not clearly Christian, that they have been derived from secular psychology and only superficially adapted for pastoral use. Professors of pastoral counseling have suspected that most of what takes place in courses on theology is irrelevant to meeting the human needs the minister is called upon to address. Unfortunately, both suspicions are too well-founded.[1]

Working as I do in an academic environment where courses are taught by specialists and where the students themselves are expected to relate their course work to their practice of ministry, I have come to the realization that this task of correlation is not only the most difficult but also one of the least addressed in seminary education.

In order for pastoral care and counseling to be more than just psychotherapy "with a twist," it must have a sound theological base that informs its theory and practice, shaping not only the way pastoral care is carried out but also the actual words a minister speaks in care-giving encounters. At the same time theology, if it is to be vital and relevant, must be informed by the needs and experiences of people and by the ministry of pastoral care.

In previous books I have commented briefly on the relationship between the two areas, but pastoral counseling and caring techniques were the first focus of those writings. In this book the correlation of pastoral care with theology is my primary concern. Both are important for faithful pastoral care and counseling to occur.

This book is certainly the most challenging one I have ever written. Its preparation has stretched me both personally and professionally over nine years. As the work was in progress it enhanced my pastoral counseling sessions and hospital visits. It forced me to ask whether my practice accords with the theology I profess, and it gave me reason to do a good deal of reading "out of my field"—an opportunity that I seized and relished.

The Word of God and Pastoral Care is offered to you, the reader, as an introduction to correlating pastoral care and theology. The "and" in the title is what concerns me. My purpose is neither a thorough elaboration of pastoral care nor a detailed exposition of systematic theology, but the meeting of the two. Assuming that all teaching aims at the developing of skill, or the gaining of knowledge, or the influencing of attitude, then this book focuses mainly on the third of these three goals. My hope is that as an introduction it will stimulate and enrich your thinking and assist you in your own endeavor to bring together these two fields.

Chapter 1 gives an overview of the state of pastoral care and counseling today, noting some of the major contemporary movements in the field. Chapter 2 focuses on pastoral assessment of the persons served, including assessment of their theological beliefs. Chapter 3 presents my theological understanding of the ministry of pastoral care and counseling. Pastoral care is not to be relegated to the fringes of ministry—as it has been by many interpreters in the history of the church—but is at the heart of the church's proclamation of the Word. Chapter 4 draws on recent neurological research into brain function in order to offer suggestions for more extensive and rigorous correlation. Chapter 5 sets forth spiritual direction as a discipline that can help our pastoral care and counseling ministry regain a solid theological base.

Succeeding chapters explore how several theological concepts might be more explicitly and intentionally related to pastoral care—the priesthood of all believers in chapter 6, acceptance of self and spirit in chapter 7, and theodicy in chapter 8. These three issues are of course only a selection, intended to be illustrative but by no means complete.

My research over these past nine years was assisted by grants from Brite Divinity School and Texas Christian University, the Division of Professional Leadership of the Lutheran Church in America, the Lutheran Brotherhood Insurance Company, and an anonymous Fort Worth donor. For all this help I am indeed grateful.

A good portion of the book was written during a research leave in 1985–86. The burden of my teaching and supervising responsibilities that year was cast on many of my colleagues at Brite, especially Marcus Bryant, and I am grateful to each of them for carrying this extra load. I am indebted to the many persons who helped in the writing effort, especially those who read all or portions of the manuscript: David Balch, Marcus Bryant, William Clements, Howard Clinebell, Jr., William Countryman, James Duke, and David Gouwens. In addition I want to express appreciation to John Schaub, with whom I coauthored the article on which chapter 3 is based, and to Edward A. Cooperrider who lent his skills to the editing of the manuscript. Carolyn Zerweck provided valuable help in research for the book. Celene Elliot prepared a careful index for the manuscript. Jean Burnham carefully typed the numerous drafts, and Karen Stone gave many hours of her time to the preparation of the text; for this help too I express my deep gratitude.

Many of the ideas presented in this book are drawn from my day-to-day clinical practice of pastoral care and counseling. Consequently, the book contains portions of actual case histories. Since confidentiality is essential to pastoral practice, all case descriptions have been altered with respect to name and other particulars in order to preserve anonymity while not distorting the essential reality of the experience described.

Howard W. Stone
The Ascension of Our Lord
Westcott House
Cambridge University
Cambridge, England

---

1. John B. Cobb, Jr., *Theology and Pastoral Care* (Philadelphia: Fortress Press, 1977), p. 1.

Introduction

The Religion Taboo

"It's just that I'm so lonely," the thirty-seven-year-old woman, recently divorced, said to her pastor. "I feel as if God is no longer there."

Pastor:	You're feeling abandoned, alone since John left you.
Counselee:	Yes, and my prayer life is a big nothing. Talking to God is like talking to the wall.
Pastor:	Not having your husband there has left you feeling very much alone.
Counselee:	Uh . . . well, yes, but I wish I could pray now and know God's will for me.
Pastor:	You want to know what to do.
Counselee:	*(Pause)* I want to know what God has in store for me. *(Pause)* I've always felt in tune with God's will, but just now I'm having trouble even knowing what to do.
Pastor:	Are you dating now?

Religion appears to have replaced sex as the major taboo among pastoral counseling ministers. At any rate it is certainly the primary taboo I encounter in my supervision of trainees in pastoral counseling. Talking about religion, using religious resources with those who come for help, or thinking theologically about their cases, makes most students feel uncomfortable and embarrassed.

When in supervised pastoral counseling a client says, "I believe it is the will of God" or "What does the Bible say about it?" or "Scripture says it's wrong, doesn't it?" the trainee often is embarrassed, stammers an evasive response, offers Rogerian mirroring, or simply ignores the "religious" comments. Or a trainee may respond with subtle but apparent condescension, as an "enlightened" counselor responding to one who is less aware. Rarely do the clients' feelings or thoughts concerning their faith meet a response as sensitive as that with which other counseling topics are discussed. This religion taboo reminds me of the skittishness about sex that I and other trainees felt a couple of decades ago, when I first began doing pastoral counseling. The dynamics are the same; only the sensitive subject has changed.

Does this anti-religion bias exist only among students and trainees? Hardly. For most of us the temptation is strong indeed, when the topic of religion comes up, to change the subject, gloss over the religious issue, and deflect the conversation by asking, "Are you dating now?"

Early in our pastoral care education most of us were taught some version of "what it means" when counselees talk about religion. They are looking outside themselves for power and rescue. They are avoiding the issues and handing their problems over to a higher authority. Or they are seeking sure and certain answers when there are none. Perhaps they are simply venting their feelings. It may be, even, a sign of psychosis.

Any of these interpretations may be true—*sometimes*, in whole or in part. But equally true is the fact that religious ideation and talk about God, prayer, and faith may be mishandled in pastoral counseling sessions because of the minister's own (perhaps unresolved) feelings about religion. The dynamics of a taboo are likely to be similar whatever the specific issue—be it death, sex, or even religion.

People who seek out pastors for care and counsel do not come merely because we are cheap, available, and generally nice people. Such considerations play their part, of course, but the reasons run deeper. Whenever I myself have been in distress, I have chosen a confidant or counselor carefully. I do not bare my soul with just anyone, nor do most people. It seems that a major reason why people in need approach a minister is their sense that somehow we pastors have a special tie with the ultimate, that we have faith resources and religious information which they themselves do not possess but which could be of help. Such feelings are often present, though rarely stated.

How can it be that religion is so often a taboo topic among pastoral carers? Whenever I question trainees about their discomfort or embarrassment when discussing religion with counselees, two answers consistently emerge. First, most pastoral care and counseling students, at least in the mainline Protestant seminaries, say they do not want to be mistaken for fundamentalists or arch-conservatives giving "pat" answers to difficult questions—a concern that surely cannot be faulted.

Second, the trainees do not want to force beliefs, even their own, on other people; they want their clients to have the freedom to believe for themselves. That too is extremely important. Surely I do not wish to be put in the same camp as the Hare Krishna missionary at the airport, or the street-corner evangelist, or that former neighbor of mine who could not have a simple conversation without haranguing the other person on matters of scripture and morality.

But are these the only alternatives—either we talk of religion and are therefore thought to be fundamentalists, or we cease speaking of religion altogether? Either we force our beliefs on others or we preserve their freedom by not speaking of religion at all. No. These are false dichotomies that are based on several erroneous assumptions. Let us look at these false assumptions more fully.

First, it is not necessarily true, as some assume, that evangelicals (or fundamentalists) always cram their brand of belief down the throats of other people. This false stereotype about religious conservatives is understandable. There is hardly an evening that I do not read in the paper about the crazy things that some right-wing religionist has said or done that day. It incenses me, even though I know I am reading about a small minority. The fact is that liberal and moderate Christians do not have a corner on the sensitivity-interpersonal-relationships market, and I know some liberals who are as dogmatic as the most rigid conservative. Only the dogma is different.

Do we have to allow arch-conservative religionists to steal our methods (and our message)? Our desire to dissociate ourselves from the televangelists of this world, who not only make the evening papers but are frequently the butt of jokes on the morning talk shows, should not make us forsake our call. Talking of faith with the faithful, using prayer and scripture in care and counseling, anointing the sick and offering the Eucharist during a hospital visit, all are part of our heritage and of our present-day pastoral care and counseling ministry.

Second, the either-or assumption is without base. Certainly there is a middle ground between forcing my beliefs onto others and saying nothing. I doubt if most of us clergy believe things because they have been forced on us; rather we accept certain ideas because they seem right. Parishioners are not of a different subspecies than pastors. People will generally hold fast to a belief because it makes sense, not because it is forced on them by a religious authority. Surely pastors can talk sensitively about religion, and even interject their own viewpoints, without being coercive. After all, our goal in pastoral counseling is to help individuals accept more fully their own humanness (and that of others) and fulfill their calling as people of God. As regards faith, we probably can exercise an influence, but surely we are not able to coerce people into believing.

Religion and religious issues can be discussed with a client in much the same way that other issues are handled. If a troubled couple see a marriage counselor they expect, and rightly so, that the counselor will draw from a well of professional experience those ideas and methods that can assist them in strengthening their marriage. The situation is similar for ministers. If people come to us as experts in issues of faith, belief, and meaning, they can anticipate, rightly, that we will speak out of our expertise in this particular area. A marriage counselor does not hand down fiats about how a given marriage should function, but carefully helps clients look, for example, at alternative patterns of female/male relationships and at different ways of structuring family discipline. Similarly, a minister does not speak in dictums but helps people look at their present understanding of God and what it means to be a child of that God and consider alternative ways of coming into contact with the One who is love.

Third, it is also risky business to assume that everyone who wants to talk about faith, or everyone who desires prayer or the Eucharist, will ask for it. Such an assumption is about as valid as telling the recently bereaved, "If there's anything I can do, please let me know." In most instances the bereaved will not ask for help. They do not want to impose. They do not even know how to ask the right questions. They are not at all sure what *will* help. What they need is the loving offer to do specific things, such as taking a son to his flute lesson, bringing in an evening meal, cleaning the house, or sharing a ride to worship. Similarly, in pastoral care and counseling we need to develop sensitivity to the various types of religious resources that may be needed in specific situations and then offer them. Of course people may say no. What is worse, they may tolerate our praying with them when deep down they would rather we did not. Such a risk exists. But since the pendulum in recent care and counseling has swung so far away from pastoral speech about God and from the use of our spiritual heritage, we need to risk erring in the other direction—all the while using our religious resources as sensitively as we use all other resources in the care process.

There is yet another assumption that sometimes hinders pastoral carers in their use of spiritual resources. It is the belief that if such resources are not helpful to me personally, they most likely will not be helpful to the people I counsel. ("If prayer is outmoded for me, it certainly will be of little use to others.") Let's face it: for many of us, what piqued our special interest in care and counseling was not only a prior interest in psychology but perhaps also some personal experience of the benefits of psychotherapy, but not everyone has had the same experiences as we. Not everyone is comfortable with the field of psychology, let alone with the thought of entering into psychotherapy. For many people, religious resources have formed the basis of their meaning in life, and returning to them can help recement a shaken foundation. Carers who discount religious resources can be denying their clients important forms of pastoral support.

A fifth assumption, often erroneous, is that religious resources should be used only after a relationship is well established. Although in general, care relationships should probably begin with long periods of listening and attending, in some situations that I have experienced, religious resources were exactly what were needed to help establish (or reestablish) the pastoral relationship from the onset.

I never will forget a recent occasion when I was called to the hospital at eleven o'clock one Sunday night by the family of an elderly woman who was comatose and not expected to live until morning. I was not the family's first choice, but their own pastor was out of town, so they called me. I had had a prior acquaintance with only two family members; I had never met the other people gathered outside that intensive care unit. After introducing ourselves and reviewing briefly the woman's condition, the ten of us sat in silence, occasionally exchanging some embarrassed small talk. After about fifteen or twenty minutes, in which I was as uncomfortable as they were, I asked whether they would like to pray. At least seven of them immediately, in unison, said, "Yes!" We prayed, and immediately everything changed. The little cluster of assorted friends suddenly became a cohesive unit. For me it became obvious that one of their unspoken reasons for inviting me was that they wanted to pray together as a group but felt unable to do so without a minister. (I could lament here about the fact that laypeople so often expect the clergy to do their praying for them—but that is hardly the point.) In this situation prayer transformed the interrelationships of the people gathered. Immediately there was a more spontaneous expression of feelings. Several people even sat back and sighed, obviously experiencing at long last a moment of peace in the midst of their difficult crisis.

The religion taboo must be confronted as surely as any other taboo we might hold. The pastoral counseling supervision I received when I was first in training compelled me to face sex as a taboo. My supervisor talked to me about it. He urged me, when counselees broached the matter, to discuss the issues openly with them rather than to change the subject; he even wanted me to initiate questions having to do with sexuality and sexual relations. He urged me to explore my own feelings about sex and the way I came to them. Such a process also can be helpful with regard to the religion taboo. We need to be aware of how we feel about it and to learn what in our background has led us to such feelings. We also need to read about it and to discuss the matter with our colleagues. We need to think and talk about it in actual practice, even bring the topic up in our dealings with parishioners. In fact, we need to view other persons' desire for religious resources not necessarily as a sign of dependency, but as a reaching out to establish or reclaim meaning in the midst of their present pain.

1. Returning to the Roots

The Babylonian Captivity of the Church, a famous Reformation treatise, offered to the church of 1520 a fresh understanding of the sacraments. In it, Martin Luther the theologian joins Martin Luther the pastor in a discussion of some of the "impediments" that had traditionally been thought to justify annulment of a marriage. Detailed consideration is given to the specific case of a woman whose husband is impotent but refuses to grant his wife a divorce. Luther suggests two alternatives:

Then I would further counsel her, with the consent of the man (who is not really her husband, but only a dweller under the same roof with her), to have intercourse with another, say her husband's brother, but to keep this marriage secret and to ascribe the children to the so-called putative father. The question is: Is such a woman saved and in a saved state? I answer: Certainly, because in this case an error, ignorance of the man's impotence, impedes the marriage; and the tyranny of the laws permits no divorce. But the woman is free through the divine law, and cannot be compelled to remain continent. Therefore the man ought to concede her right, and give up to somebody else the wife who is his only in outward appearance.

Moreover, if the man will not give his consent, or agree to this separation—rather than allow the woman to burn [I Cor. 7:9] or to commit adultery—I would counsel her to contract a marriage with another and flee to a distant unknown place. What other counsel can be given to one constantly struggling with the dangers of natural emotions? . . . Is not the sin of a man who wastes his wife's body and life a greater sin than that of the woman who merely alienates the temporal goods of her husband?[1]

Today, blessed with learnings from modern psychology that were unavailable to Luther, we can chuckle over the pastoral care he suggests for the wife of an impotent husband. Luther's proposed resolution of the problem, however, allowing the wife either to have sexual relations with a relative of the husband or to run off to another city with a new husband, at least represented an honest attempt to understand pastoral care from a theological standpoint—the perspective of Christian liberty.

Today, a couple seeking pastoral help for this same problem is likely to learn of additional alternatives, perhaps some of the highly effective therapeutic methods that are currently available. A theological understanding that sends the wife packing to Billings or Paducah with a new husband would be clearly inadequate. The techniques offered by such specialists as Masters and Johnson can be of real help to individuals and couples trying to cope with sexual dysfunction.[2]

For those of us who live and work at the interface between theology and pastoral care, however, a new dilemma has arisen. Along with the tremendous benefits that psychology has brought to modern society, to the church, and to ministers doing pastoral care, there also has come an attendant loss. In our actual care of persons we have tended to ignore the basic foundations and full heritage of Christian care throughout the ages; we have tended to ignore our biblical heritage in theology, ethics, and anthropology. In fact, as I mentioned in the "Introduction," religion seems at times to have replaced sex as the major taboo among pastoral carers.

It would seem that pastoral care in recent decades has actually lost its roots. Enthralled by the truly impressive strides made by other scholarly disciplines in our time, it has cut itself off from the historical tradition of church and theology, in at least two important respects: (1) pastoral care has become identified so largely with pastoral counseling as to forget the larger meaning of care in its historically more encompassing aspects, and (2) it has come to accept certain implied values and concepts of humanity in secular mental health practice, thereby loosening its historic ties to Christian theology.

The Historical Breadth of Pastoral Care

In a brilliant historical analysis William Clebsch and Charles Jaeckle point to four functions of pastoral care in the Christian tradition. Pastoral care is understood historically to embrace the helping acts performed by representative Christians as they facilitate the healing, sustaining, guiding, and reconciling of troubled individuals, persons whose difficulties occur within the context of ultimate meanings and concerns.[3] All four of these traditional functions are important.

Healing is the pastoral function that "aims to overcome some impairment by restoring a person to wholeness and by leading him to advance beyond his previous condition."[4] Historically the function of healing has been carried out through such acts an anointing, exorcism, prayers to the saints, pilgrimages to shrines, charismatic healing, magic, and magic medicine.

Sustaining is the function that helps individuals endure and rise above situations in which a restoration to their previous condition is unlikely. Church history records perseverance, consolation, and visitation of the sick and shut-ins as ways in which this function has been exercised.

The guiding function consists of "assisting perplexed persons to make confident choices . . . when such choices are viewed as affecting the present and future state of the soul."[5] Throughout the centuries two basic forms of guidance have been used in pastoral care. "Inductive guidance" leads the persons cared for to adopt *a priori* sets of values as the basis for making decisions. "Eductive guidance" elicits from people's own lives and values the criteria for decision-making. Historically, pastoral guidance has been primarily inductive, at various times involving devil-craft, advice-giving, spiritual direction, and listening.

The fourth function, reconciling, seeks to reestablish

broken relationships between persons and between individuals and God. Historically, the function of reconciliation has involved such activities as forgiveness, discipline, penance, confession, and absolution.

Pastoral Care in the Twentieth Century

Pastoral care in our century has emphasized primarily eductive guiding, with a secondary emphasis on the healing of the psyche. With the rise of pastoral counseling as the queen of pastoral care functions, eductive guidance has in fact all but displaced the other three functions of sustaining, healing, and reconciling. Today in the pastoral care movement, and especially in the United States, I see three major approaches to pastoral care and counseling that dominate the scene: the traditional method, emphasizing inductive guidance; the nondirective approach, emphasizing eductive guidance; and the revised model, emphasizing all four functions.

A pastor from my hometown routinely uses the first method. He frequently has criticized me for the amounts of time I spend in care and counseling with a given individual and tells me he is able to accomplish most of his pastoral counseling in just one visit. A couple comes to him with a marriage problem. He opens his Bible and reads several pertinent verses showing that the wife is to be submissive to her husband. Then he prays with them thanking God that they know where to find the solution to their problem. This pastor claims that he has actually cured many marriages this way, since (small wonder) few ever have returned for a second session! This admittedly extreme example can perhaps serve to illustrate the traditional approach to pastoral care, one that many of us inherited.

This traditional method has its advantages. It is quick. It uses religious resources and builds on the community's residual acceptance of pastoral authority. It deals with the family system as a whole. It is action-oriented. Yet for all its emphasis on inductive guidance—telling people on the basis of scripture what they have to do—this method falls short, because there is no listening to a person's pain, little learning from the positive benefits of modern psychology, and little opportunity for individuals to grapple their own way through to needed solutions of their unique problems.

In reaction to this traditional approach a new method of pastoral care came on the scene in the forties and fifties. Relying mainly on Carl Rogers, with a smattering of Freud, it became known as the nondirective approach. This method emphasized such things as the structured fifty-minute interview, the role of unconscious motivation in human behavior, the childhood basis of most adult responses, and insight as the major goal of counseling.

The nondirective approach came to the field of pastoral care like a breath of fresh air. It has many advantages. Pastors are trained to talk less and listen more to the pain of the people they encounter; this helps establish rapport and build a solid pastor-parishioner relationship. The lessons of modern psychology are taken seriously. Many of the negative aspects of ministerial authority long associated with the *Herr Pastor* image are avoided.

Despite its obvious advantages over the earlier model, however, the nondirective approach too has its liabilities. The major difficulty is that it focuses almost exclusively on one form of pastoral care—eductive guidance, with its techniques of listening and uncovering, its emphasis on insight as the goal of pastoral care—while ignoring cognitions and behavior.[6] Other disadvantages worth mentioning are its time-consuming interest in exploring past events, its penchant for the fifty-minute hour as the preferred setting, and its tendency to look more at individuals than at full family systems.[7]

A revised model made its appearance in 1966 with the publication of one of the most important books that had yet appeared—Howard Clinebell's *Basic Types of Pastoral Counseling*.[8] Clinebell acknowledged the contributions of the nondirective model, but he also cautioned that if allowed to stand alone or taken as the sole model, it would greatly limit the opportunities otherwise inherent in the office of pastor.

Clinebell went a long way toward helping pastors return to the historical elements of pastoral care, but now there is both the need and the possibility to go even further. Clinebell's approach still tended to focus more on counseling than on care. His methods were still tied in large measure to eductive guidance. There was little impetus or direction for correlating the moral and theological tradition with the pastoral care process (although Clinebell, it must be noted, has been a major proponent of social-ethical concerns).

The New Shape of Pastoral Care

In an effort to help incorporate the historic tradition into present and future practice, I would propose here ten theses suggestive of the shape that pastoral care for the parish can take today. These theses, of course, draw upon both the traditional and the nondirective models, and especially upon Clinebell's revised model, but they attempt also to more fully integrate the four historical functions of pastoral care.[9]

1. Pastoral care recognizes liturgy, ritual, confession, and traditional and contemporary Christian resources as beneficial components. It is not shy of offering prayers and sound spiritual healing for the sick. It draws from the discipline of spiritual direction. It reemphasizes the work of the Spirit.

2. Pastoral care does not view personality change as the primary goal of its work. Sometimes it is supportive of the person, at other times it is confrontive; sometimes it fosters renewal of relationships, at other times it facilitates their ending. At all times it helps people stretch to use to the full their God-given resources and strengths, while at the same time recognizing that persons are finite and that the source of all growth lies outside themselves. Finally, it recognizes that the pastoral care goal of all Christians is growth in the faith and loving service to others.

3. Pastoral care is not morally or theologically neutral. It operates from a Christian perspective and, when appropriate and effective, speaks to the parishioner from this perspective. It incorporates within it moral guidance and spiritual

direction. In short, pastoral care does not stop at teaching the skills of effective living; it points also to a moral life, a faithful life of service to neighbor. There is ongoing engagement in the task of correlating theology and pastoral care.

4. Pastoral care occurs within a Christian context—the "community of saints." It attempts to incorporate those who are cared for into the church. It seeks to bridge the gap between people and the gap between alienated individuals and God.

5. Pastoral care is not performed only by the pastor. It is a task also for the laity. Taking seriously Luther's belief in the priesthood of all believers, it empowers the laity to strengthen the caring done in and by a congregation.

6. Pastoral care has a systemic and social orientation. Although pastoral care is not the same as social change, it is informed—as surely as any other aspect of the church's ministry—by an awareness of the need for social action in specific situations.

7. Where pastoral care calls for pastoral counseling, frequently in response to a crisis, that counseling normally is short term, perhaps six to eight sessions or even fewer. If counseling must take longer, counselees usually are referred to professionals or to agencies within the community.

8. Pastoral care takes seriously the pastor's task and opportunity for initiation. It does not stand idly by waiting for people to request a counseling session. It takes the risk, once a problem is seen, of offering care even where help has not been sought. It is proactive, not simply reactive to expressed needs.

9. Pastoral care aims to help people develop not only their feelings and attitudes, but also constructive behaviors and thinking. It recognizes that to a great extent what a person feels and does is dependent upon what that individual thinks and believes.

10. Finally, pastoral care focuses on coping with contemporary here-and-now issues rather than on extensive analysis of past history. Its orientation is preventive, centered on the strengthening of existing skills, abilities, and relationships rather than on breaking down or uncovering deep-seated problems or defects.

The model of pastoral care here proposed involves all four strands of the tradition. The future health of pastoral care and counseling itself depends in larger measure on our regaining the historic balance and interaction between healing, sustaining, guiding, and reconciling.

Theology and Pastoral Care

Pastoral care has benefited greatly by the twentieth-century strides made in psychology. Unwittingly, however, it also has adopted some of the values and concepts of humanity—the "theologies"—of modern psychology, thereby loosening its ties to Christian theology.[10] When pastoral care is faithful to its historical tradition, it is not theologically or morally neutral, as most psychotherapies claim to be, but seeks to help people grow in effective Christian living. When it is not, it is virtually indistinguishable, in philosophy and in function, from modern psychotherapeutic practice.

Over the past two decades I have had occasion to review thousands of case histories and audio and video tapes of pastoral care and counseling sessions. These sessions seem to be characterized by one major and striking feature: theological constructs exert little influence on the help being offered. The pastor's beliefs about sin, grace, judgment, and forgiveness apparently have little effect on the meeting between pastor and parishioner. Why? Are the ministers so poorly trained? The problem is not that simply stated. A more likely reason is that pastoral care (and especially pastoral counseling) has often adopted the "theologies" implicit in modern psychotherapies and hence drawn away from its own roots in the message of Christian theology.

The Secular "Theologies"

This unwitting embrace of secular mental health presuppositions has two consequences. In the first place, the emphasis on eductive guidance by the nondirective pastoral care movement has led the pastor to adopt a more neutral stance toward issues of value and meaning. Eductive counseling does not impose on the person in need an outside moral ethic or theological solution, but attempts to clarify and reshape the emotional responses of parishioners within their own value framework. Practitioners of psychotherapy have rightly noted that if a counselor is judgmental when trying to establish rapport, the counseling process comes to a sudden halt. Building rapport requires that the counselor be warm, open, relaxed, and suspend judgment. But by adopting the neutral stance of the secular counselor, ministers have often lost sight of their task as spiritual directors, ethicists, and theologians. Our pastoral care has leaned toward "bearing one another's burdens," while relegating the work of judgment to the sermon, or politics, or social concerns. Pastoral care has lost that tension between law and gospel, judgment and grace, of which Luther spoke so forcefully.

In the second place, there is no real neutrality anyway among the mental health care providers. The concept of humanity implicit in much psychology today (especially humanistic psychology) has a much more positive image of human beings than does a Christian anthropology that recognizes the existence of sin in the world. In this regard I am reminded especially of Luther's understanding of the person as simultaneously both saint and sinner. Most humanistic psychologies, and many others as well, focus mainly on the saint in each of us; they do not recognize the sinner. They thus ignore our human finitude.

Most psychological theorists and system-builders in our century have hidden behind the guise of "scientific neutrality." The truth is, though, that their psychotherapies are not neutral! There is a reason why some psychotherapies tend to set themselves against mores and culture. There is a reason why some types of marriage counseling result in a greater number of divorces than others. Those reasons have to do with underlying value assumptions.

Many therapies, besides describing what the "actualized"

or "ideal" person is to be, also detail how life is to be lived. They define what health and happiness are. They spell out the marks of love. But these matters all involve questions of meaning, and any system that addresses them is functioning like a religion.

In many ways psychology has become the new religion. Its ministers purvey its teachings through encounter groups, psychotherapy, pop psychology books, and talk shows. They zealously evangelize for EST, TA, Rolfing, Gestalt, and Primal Scream. The consequence is that when pastoral care is cut adrift from its traditional roots, when it adopts exclusively the eductive method of guidance, these secular "theologies," rather than Christian theology, become the base from which pastoral care and counseling is conceived and practiced.

The Mental Health Ethic

Some years ago in a paper entitled "The Mental Health Ethic" I suggested that what was then being required of people by the various psychotherapies was tantamount to a rejection of the Christian ethic in favor of a new one. Uncertain about my thesis, I shared the paper with some of my colleagues. They were unconvinced, even bemused. I filed my paper away and did not look at it again until recently.

The mental health ethic I then described is even more prevalent today. It varies from one school of thought and practice to another—from one ideology to another, if you will. But there also are some common themes: Be open and honest. Be warm. Do what you feel ("Go with your feelings"). Be congruent. Be assertive. Share your innermost feelings. Be in touch with your sexuality. I'm okay, you're okay. Get out of your mind and into your feelings. Pull your own strings.

Now there is much to be said for most of these admonitions, and the qualities extolled are at least somewhat honorable. Their apologists, however, tend often to be one-sided, studiously avoiding a fully developed Christian ethic. Pastors who segregate the caring portion of their ministry from the rest of ministry, who do pastoral care as if they were not ministers, or even Christians, need to have their consciousness raised to the significant differences that exist between pastoral care and the secular care offered in such other disciplines as psychotherapy and social work. Essentially these differences can be reduced to matters of perspective and of context.[11]

The Distinctiveness of Christian Care

The first thing that makes pastoral counseling unique is the perspective of the pastor. Ministers, of course, use various methods borrowed from secular psychology, but we approach them within a specific theological framework. Christian theology is distinctive in its perspective on what it means to be human, its concept of health, its understanding of human plight and rescue. It often perceives in the suffering person's words a different struggle and end point. This means that the warmth, openness, and acceptance of the pastor in any pastoral care relationship takes on transcendent meaning. A sound theological perspective influences the whole warp and woof of pastoral care.

A second difference between pastors and secular counselors derives from the fact that pastoral care occurs within the context of the Christian community. The minister-parishioner encounter in a counseling chamber has as its larger setting the community of the church—a faith community. This context in fact is not just a particular congregation at one point in time but a long pastoral care tradition embracing the whole church and bridging the generations since at least the first century. This recognition that pastoral care occurs within the "community of saints" helps guard against the privatism or pietism that has often affected secular psychotherapy.

Thus there is something different about pastoral care, and this "difference" means that the minister who responds to individuals from a Christian perspective and within the context of the Christian community must have grappled with and be working out a theology of such things as sexuality, marriage, reconciliation, health, and death. Theology books and courses are not dry theoretical exercises involving pie-in-the-sky formulations that have no human reference; they help establish the foundations for pastoral care ministry.

Roadblocks to Correlation

It has been said that one distinctive aspect of pastors' care is their perspective, the way they correlate theology with their pastoral practice. There are a number of problems, though, inherent in this correlation of theology and pastoral care. Assuming we agree that such a correlation should occur, and aside from the methodological issues yet to be discussed as to how that can be done, there are basic difficulties than can hinder any such meeting and interaction. A familiarity with these difficulties alerts the carer to potential roadblocks thwarting the much-needed dialogue. The major trouble spots deserve listing.

A first area of conflict involves the matter of territorial rights. Who owns the correlation enterprise? Which "side" gets to speak first—or last? Michael Taylor refers to this as disagreement over the game plan: Who serves first? What is in or out of bounds? How it is scored? What is the agenda?[12] When there are differences, how do we go about settling them? What is the final authority? Scripture? Tradition? Experience? Relevance? You probably remember from seminary days the tensions between the practical and classical fields. Those tensions, and the attendant egos and politics, come into play when the two fields meet.

A second problem involves the question of which theology pastoral care is supposed to relate to. Should it be correlated with one of our historical theologies or a contemporary

theology? Which of the contemporary theologies—all of
them, some of them, or only one? A denominational
theology? There are so many voices, so many languages, so
many historical periods of varying theological concern.

Further, which pastoral care approach is to take part in the
dialogue? Earlier in this chapter I sketched out the shape
pastoral care should take in ministry today, but is my sketch
sufficient? One of the things I have learned in my travels, and
especially on an extended research leave in Great Britain, is
that there are many diverse understandings of pastoral care
in our world today. Which one is to take the lead in the
much-needed dialogue?

Another related concern is the issue of which school of
psychology (if any) underlies the pastoral care. Psychoanaly-
sis and nondirective psychotherapy, as we know, are not the
only ones that can influence pastoral care. A review of books
on pastoral care and counseling in the last several decades
will reveal that pastoral care has drawn heavily from a host of
schools, including Jung, Psychosynthesis, Transactional
Analysis, Integrity Therapy, Gestalt Therapy, cognitive
therapy, systems marriage and family counseling, behavioral
therapy, and Reality Therapy. Contrast orthodox Freudian-
ism with Rational-Emotive Therapy and you will see that the
pastoral care which relies on one psychological theory will
look quite different from that which relies on another. And in
either event, to what extent do you allow any particular
therapeutic approach to determine the pastoral care offered?

If this dilemma is not sufficiently discouraging, read on.
The plot thickens. The understanding of ministry varies
considerably from person to person, from denomination to
denomination, from one period of history to another. I
happen to be keenly interested in the great pastoral carers of
previous centuries, in how they did their care; from them I
learn more about how I do mine. Edward Pusey and John
Keble of the Oxford Movement, for example, were both
sensitive, caring, compassionate priests; their letters demon-
strate great concern for others in distress. But their
paternalism and relatively authoritarian understanding of
the office of the priesthood, especially as it relates to

confession, would not be acceptable to most ministers today. So too among modern clerics is considerable diversity in the concept of ministry and the role of the minister.

Another difficulty in correlating theology and pastoral care has to do with the extreme complexity of the human beings who are the subjects of care. When we begin to relate theology and pastoral care in concrete situations—with reference to the specific people we encounter—we find that humans are very complex beings. No two carers would ever agree completely about given clients: who they are, what their needs are, and what motivates their behavior. There are simply too many unknowns in our knowing, too many uncertainties about the individuals we seek to help, too much that is shrouded in mystery.

Yet another difficulty: when correlating theology and pastoral care, which doctrines do we consider? It is my impression that some doctrines of the church—anthropology, ministry, soteriology—relate quite readily to the types of situations we encounter in the day-in and day-out practice of pastoral ministry. Others, such as those that speak of the garden or the last things may seem distant and of little value. Which doctrines are to take priority in the process of correlation? Which are to form the starting point of our theology?

Finally, do we consider laypersons as pastoral carers? If so, that will change the character of the task as well. For then we will need to develop for the carer lacking a seminary education a method of correlation that will not be so inordinately difficult or obscure as to be useless, yet will not be so simplistic as to avoid the complexities of the actual enterprise.

Incorporating the Theological into Pastoral Care

There is a way out of this morass, muddled though it may seem. What is required is that we be prepared, do the necessary spadework, and reflect on our experience in light of the Word. In that way theology can have an impact on our care. We may not, and probably cannot, resolve all the difficulties just enumerated, but we can be sensitive to them and hold them in tension as we proceed with the task of correlation. We can also recognize that what we finally come up with is likely to be very time-bound and situation-bound, perhaps applying to only one specific individual or at best to one particular community.

We shall refer to chapter 2 to the beginnings of a methodology for correlating theology and pastoral care and to chapter 4 for a way to do it, but at this point I would simply call attention to some of the issues involved. I see the correlation process actually occurring in concrete situations, perhaps in such pastoral acts as visiting an accident victim in the hospital, counseling an estranged couple, or calling on a lonely widower.

Picture this for a simple example: The doorbell rings and when you answer it the paper boy barks, "Collect!" You leave him on the step, run to the bedroom, and return with a ten-dollar bill, apologizing, "Sorry, I don't have anything smaller." "That's okay, I've got it here," and he gives you a handful of bills and coins in change. You wish him a good evening. On the way back to your bedroom you casually count the money in your hand and realize that he gave you change for a twenty instead of a ten. What do you do? Without a moment's hesitation you probably run to the door and call him back before he gets too far down the street. You explain that he gave you ten dollars too much and he blurts out a surprised, "Thanks a lot!" before going on his way.

Why did you decide to return the money? You could have kept it—most ministers probably have need of some extra change. The boy's mistake had confronted you with an ethical dilemma. Without even weighing alternatives you made a choice. Not everyone would instinctively call the paper boy back in such a situation; in fact, many people would not. Your decision had to be based on something prior, something more than a general free-floating niceness in your nature. Your response was doubtless shaped in the distant past, by values you had long ago learned or grew to hold important. These values and beliefs were probably heightened by your years in seminary, and by subsequent study of scripture as you prepared for preaching and teaching. In addition, these values have been shaped by your own exploration of what it is to be a faithful servant; they have come from the examination of your life and the values you live by. Such beliefs are part and parcel of your faith. You might not be able to articulate them as well as you would like, but your faith and values at times overrule the possibility of some responses, such as the urge to think, "Oh, what's the difference, he has no debts, no mouths to feed, and maybe he will learn something from the loss."

The correlation of pastoral care with theology, though it sounds frightfully like an academic exercise, needs to proceed almost as automatically in the concrete care situation as in your response to the paper boy. (See chapter 4 for its discussion of how the brain's two hemispheres assist the correlation process.) Although you will occasionally have the luxury of reflecting on the care you offer, good correlation happens over and over again almost automatically in the way you listen and respond to another's anguish. Our faith, beliefs, and values shape what we say and do, how we respond.

Sound easy? I'm afraid there is a catch. Most pastoral care situations are more complex than the case of the paper boy. Competing values are likely to be involved—one's own ego needs, unexamined assumptions induced by the media, the inadequate values inherent in contemporary psychology, pressures from family and friends and even the bishop. Indeed the competition is so great that it becomes easy for us in pastoral situations to respond not according to Christian values, but according to our own narcissism or professional pride or the mores of society.

For authentic correlation to occur, the pastor must return over and over again to the primary texts that shape the faith. An ethics course back in seminary may have prepared us well enough for the dilemma of the paper boy, but it may not sufficiently alert pastors to the dangers of an increasing emotional involvement with and dependency on a counselee of the opposite sex. So, for correlation to occur, the pastor must repeatedly return to the sources of the faith, read widely in theology and ethics, and have a continuing dialogue with the competing value and belief systems present in our culture.

Besides a continual return to the sources, reflection on present experience also is required. The pastor must reflect not only on former learnings, but also on recent events, indeed upon the care that is currently being given. (Chapter 4 offers suggestions on how this can be done.) It is easy for one's theological beliefs to become separated from the material world in which one works. A calm review of experience as it relates to the sources of faith, the people who are being cared for, and one's day-to-day relationship with God is essential if there is to be any ongoing encounter between theology and pastoral care.

Reflection is insufficient, however, if it is done in isolation, outside a communal context. Whether it occurs at the local ministers' weekly breakfast, under the guidance of a spiritual director or pastoral care supervisor, during dialogue and feedback within the congregation, or in intimate talks with friends and family members, the correlation of pastoral care and theology does not develop only from reviewing our private beliefs as individuals, or even the opinions of theologians and writers in pastoral care. It is ultimately formed by the convictions of the community of faith.

To summarize, each person's correlation of pastoral care and theology will involve first a study of the sources of our faith and how they are expressed in theology, and second, a reflection on those sources as well as on our present experience with people entrusted to our care and reflection on our relationship with God. Such reflection always is tied to the Christian community.

Ministers must develop a method of correlation that best suits their own needs. No two will be exactly alike. The method must be so simple that it can be absorbed and acted upon almost without thinking, and yet so sophisticated that it takes seriously the complexity of individuals, values, and beliefs. In some situations we may indeed have time to think, consult, and devise appropriate pastoral strategies; we can, for example, probably consider at length a plan of treatment for someone who is chronically depressed. But in other situations we may have to act reflexively, in a way that is comparable to the "muscle memory" we employ while driving a car or playing softball; at such times we must trust that the word resides within us, that the faith is so ingrained in our living as to affect our decisions even when we do not have opportunity to think them through.

No correlation is perfect and valid for every situation. We must continually make judgments and act upon them, but these judgments and acts remain our frail attempts at truth. They are necessarily tentative; they must remain open to critique, to correction from the community, to further insight. Nevertheless, pursuing truth to the best of our ability, we must make real commitments. It is there at the point of commitment where reflection ends and the practice of pastoral care and counseling begins. Since at the point of action there is usually not enough time to go through a complicated procedure of correlating theology with pastoral care, a "trenches hermeneutic" is required, an intuitive approach to the pastoral task. (In chapter 4 we shall further consider how this can occur.)

We are there. We act. If there has been prior reflection on theology and pastoral care, it will inform our practice. As we are attentive to the word, Christian faith will have its impact on the care we give.

NOTES

1. *Luther's Works*, American ed., vol. 36 (Philadelphia and St. Louis: Fortress Press and Concordia Publishing House, 1955–), pp. 103-4 (hereinafter cited as LW).

2. Considerably less technical than the pioneering work by William H. Masters and Virginia E. Johnson, *Human Sexual Inadequacy* (Boston: Little, Brown & Co., 1970), is the useful little "Pocket Counsel Books" volume by David Mace, *Sexual Difficulties in Marriage* (Philadelphia: Fortress Press, 1972).

3. William A. Clebsch and Charles R. Jaekle, *Pastoral Care in Historical Perspective* (Northvale, N.J.: Jason Aronson, 1964), p. 4.

4. Ibid., p. 33.

5. Ibid., p. 9.

6. My own book *Using Behavioral Methods in Pastoral Counseling* (Philadelphia: Fortress Press, 1980) is an attempt to correct this tendency to rely on only one primary form of psychotherapy in the practice of pastoral care.

7. On the systems approach to pastoral care see E. Mansell Pattison, *Pastor and Parish: A Systems Approach* (Philadelphia: Fortress Press, 1977) and, as applied to families, Douglas A. Anderson, *New Approaches to Family Pastoral Care* (Philadelphia: Fortress Press, 1980).

8. Howard Clinebell, *Basic Types of Pastoral Counseling* (Nashville: Abingdon Press, 1966), pp. 27-38.

9. The theoretical justification for these theses is drawn from a number of sources, especially, Don S. Browning, *The Moral Context of Pastoral Care* (Philadelphia: Westminster Press, 1976) and *Practical Theology* (New York: Harper & Row, 1982); Alastair Campbell, *Rediscovering Pastoral Care* (London: Darton, Longman & Todd, 1981); Howard Clinebell, *Basic Types of Pastoral Counseling* and *Growth Counseling* (Nashville: Abingdon Press, 1966, 1979); Gerard Egan, *The Skilled Helper*, 2nd ed. (Monterey, Calif.: Brooks/Cole Publishing Co., 1982); Paul A. Hauck, *Reason in Pastoral Counseling* (Philadelphia: Westminster Press, 1972); Thomas Oden, *Pastoral Theology* (New York: Harper & Row, 1983); Howard W. Stone, *Crisis Counseling* (Philadelphia: Fortress Press, 1976); and *The Caring Church: A Guide for Lay Pastoral Care* (New York: Harper & Row, 1983).

10. My colleague Marcus Bryant has rightly noted that in recent years the theological seminary has been the one counterforce to this trend.

11. See Howard W. Stone, *Suicide and Grief* (Philadelphia: Fortress Press, 1972), pp. 93-94.

12. Michael Taylor, *Learning to Care: Christian Reflections on Pastoral Practice* (London: S.P.C.K., 1983), pp. 4-5.

2. *Theological Assessment*

Imagine the scene. Two pastors are animatedly discussing a parishioner with whom one has been counseling. We get in on that part of the conversation where Pastor Phyllis concludes that Pastor Fred's parishioner is "obviously struggling with an endogenous depression exacerbated by low self-esteem . . . he is definitely moving out of an 'I'm not okay, you're okay' position, and if only he can strengthen his adult, he will reach greater wholeness."

Fred nods his assent: "I agree with your analysis of the man's script. . . . His weak ego state is related to the fact that he had a father who was an alcoholic, and he never experienced a relationship of basic trust with either parent."

Overhearing their assessment of a counselee receiving pastoral care, we begin to wonder if we are perhaps at a convention of the American Psychological Association or the Academy for the Advancement of Psychotherapy instead of at a gathering of ministers. How do pastors assess the parishioners in their care? Do we construe and interpret their problems in the categories of contemporary psychology, or is our pastoral assessment rather in terms of the church's theological tradition?

The Theological Template

The human mind seems to have within it indispensable structures that organize and interpret data received by the senses. Psychologists using a Rorschach test, for example, know that the brain organizes the ink-blot design and interprets it in the light of a client's emotional and intellectual status; for one person the multi-shaped form brings to mind a beautiful mountain scene, while for another the same shape reveals genitalia. These organizing structures of the mind, which I shall call templates, are essential for organizing information into a manageable whole.

Through years of education, training, and reflection upon experience the physician acquires a "medical template," without which a diagnosis would be impossible. A patient comes into the office and uses common, ordinary words to describe certain symptoms: "I have been feeling light-headed lately, mostly when I am standing." The physician recalls having previously prescribed medication for high blood pressure, and so responds by asking a few questions in equally simple and easily understood language, questions about body positions and movements, fatigue, stress, hearing.

When it comes to actually assessing the patient's symptoms, however, the physician moves away from ordinary language and resorts to a "medical template" learned long ago in medical school. Technical terms and highly professional categories spring readily to mind, without any need for conscious recall. There are "indications and contraindications" relative to alternative anti-hypertensive drugs, revised dosage levels to be considered, "orthostatic hypotension" and so forth. The whole bag of analytical terms and descriptive categories constitutes a "medical template" that the physician then places on both the patient's own words and the doctor's clinical observations. The purpose is to determine if the prescribed drug is working properly or if too high a dosage is producing unwelcome side effects. The medical template functions to organize the physician's observations and thinking, thus ensuring a more accurate diagnosis and appropriate treatment.

Other professionals too use templates forged from the body of terms and knowledge that is unique to their particular discipline. Each such template represents a distinctive way of looking at things, a distinct perspective on reality. None of these diverse perspectives, however, is to be regarded as final and definitive in the sense of having summarized and exhausted all possible interpretations and meanings. Even the collectivity of templates—the whole range of possible perspectives for organizing data in the mind—could not do that.

To suggest that each profession does and should use its own distinctive template is not to suggest that only one template should ever be used. The physician may use several—psychological, sociological, legal, religious—other than the strictly medical template in coming to an understanding of the patient's condition. But good physicians are not likely to reject or ignore the template they were specifically, and uniquely, trained to use.

In our "post–Christian" era, unfortunately, it seems that the pastor's template has become even more confused than those of the physician and psychologist. Religious conceptuality seems to have lost much of its intellectual credibility. Specifically religious language is rarely used any more except by conservative and fundamentalist Christians. Mainline Protestant and Catholic ministers often avoid it for fear of appearing less credible or of being associated with the religious "right wing." Because of this credibility issue many pastors are tempted to discard the theological template altogether in favor of a more contemporary secular template, such as that of psychology. Regrettable in that development is not the pastoral use of such other templates, but the exclusion of a theological template from pastoral care.

Phyllis and Fred (if in fact they did not go on to assess Fred's parishioner theologically) had in a sense sold their theological birthright for a psychological template. In this respect they do not stand alone. At times we have all done the same thing, and we continue to struggle with just such a temptation. It often seems easier to speak in Freudian terms, or in the words of Transactional Analysis, for example, than to use a theological template in our pastoral assessment.

Clearly there is a need today for the pastor in a self-conscious way, to regain a theological template that will be unique to pastoral care. Without such a template, spiritual assessment of a troubled parishioner will surely remain confused, frequently resulting in an inadequate *pastoral* response.

A theological template does not mean a rigid formula, a conceptual framework that is fixed and inflexible. It means simply a way of organizing the pastor's reflection about what has happened and is happening to the parishioner. Such a framework can help the pastor build on past experiences in working with people who have had similar difficulties. It can be a help for correlating one's theology with one's pastoral acts in concrete situations. Such integration does not imply the mechanical process of simply applying a preexisting body of doctrine to the specific care situation; it implies rather the dynamic process of actualizing our theology anew in every moment of conflict and suffering. How this can be done is the subject of the fourth chapter where it is suggested that both hemispheres of the brain with their unique methods of cognitively encoding data are required for the correlation process between a theological template and the concrete pastoral situation.

Pastoral assessment can and should be done from a theological template. The method here to be described involves the use of a series of questions—which could, of course, vary in number and content—in which the form or structure of the series is the important thing. It is offered in the hope that all pastors will be encouraged to use some theological template in their pastoral assessment.

A Method of Pastoral Assessment

Paul Pruyser has helped us affirm the unique perspective of the pastor in the assessment of persons.[1] His insights have increased our self-conscious grappling with pastoral assessment and driven us explicitly to identify various criteria that were otherwise only implicit in the formation of our pastoral judgments. The questions—wonderings—that arise in the back of our mind as we encounter people in pastoral care or counseling are not queries for the troubled person to address; they are simply constituent elements in a framework that can help ministers reach a theological understanding of what is happening. We pastors need to ask these or comparable questions of *ourselves* as we listen to the story any particular individual has to tell. If we can begin to answer these questions, we should have a better and fuller grasp of the pastoral situation we are encountering.

1. *Why is this person coming to me for help?*

There is a reason why people choose a pastor rather than a doctor, friend, attorney, mate, neighbor, relative, or colleague. When someone comes to you, it is important for you to understand *why* he or she has come specifically to you, of all people, to share a personal burden. What specifically do you symbolize to this person? Perhaps there has already developed, at least in part, the insight that the agonizing problem is basically a spiritual problem, and that surely one can turn to a pastor for help in dealing with a specifically spiritual concern.

2. *How does this person understand God?*

God is likely to be a focal concern in connection with any spiritual problem. Two aspects of that concern are addressed in this single question.

First, how does this person picture God? What is the prevailing God-concept? Is God thought of primarily as a punitive, capricious, moralistically judgmental, indifferent, distant, uncaring deity; or is God a loving, forgiving, fair, and caring parent who incorporates both judgment and grace? Often parishioners will give us insight into their view of God by the questions they ask: "Why me?" "Am I being punished?" "How could God allow this to happen to a person so young and so good?" "Why does God let her suffer so?" Questions of this sort often reveal a serious personal struggle to understand how God acts or to find meaning within the situation. They can also provide a clue to the maturity of the person and of that person's understanding of God and self.

Second, we must look not only for what the person *says* about God, but also for the congruence, or lack of congruence, between the statement and actual behavior. Is the God talked about the one to whom allegiance is really given? Where do the ultimate loyalties lie? Although some parishioners may verbalize easily about the God we encounter in Jesus Christ, their behavior may indicate that they actually worship money instead—or sex or power or work or anything else that is less than ultimate but nonetheless demands and receives their major concern and devotion. The pastor needs to ask, What is the primary value about which this person's life is centered?

3. *What is the sense of sin and what role does sin play in this situation?*

The root meaning and cause of sin for Augustine, as for Paul, is idolatry: we worship the gift rather than the Giver. The question about sin, again, has two aspects.

First, what is this individual's sense of sin, if any? Does guilt appear to be present? If so, does the guilt refer to identifiable wrongs actually committed, or does it reflect something more general—feelings of unworthiness, a self-deprecating attitude? Does the individual accept personal responsibility or shift the blame to some scapegoat? Is the person's awareness of sin experienced only as a sense of shame or remorse, or does it involve also, in the biblical sense, repentance, the intention to change for the better?

Second, what is the impact of "corporate" sin on this situation? Is the person being deformed or destroyed by group, communal, or societal structures that oppress and dehumanize? Is the individual experiencing social injustice? Is she suffering from the effects of sexual stereotyping and prejudice simply because she is a woman? The pastor must attend to the individual sin on the one hand, and to societal evil on the other, discerning the impact of each on the individual.

4. *What is this person's relative capacity for faith?*

Often it is assumed that every person has a completely

adequate capacity for faith. In a sense this is true, for no one is beyond God's ability to reach. It may be overly optimistic, however, for the pastor to assert, "All you need is to have faith."

The depressed teenage boy who was extensively abused as a child and has never lived in one home for more than two years may not sense that the world is indeed hospitable and the people in it good. He may believe that the only good is what he gets for himself, that all of creation is primarily evil, that no one can be trusted. The scarring that has occurred in such a life should not be ignored or taken lightly.

It would be a tragedy, of course, if all capacity for faith were to be denied. Almost as bad, however, is the easy idealism that embraces unreal expectations for the growth of faith.

5. *How does this person view salvation?*

Salvation is the central promise of the Christian faith. But how does this particular person view it?

Luther noted that Christian faith lives *sola gratia, sola fide*—by grace alone, by faith alone. He pointed to Paul's claim that salvation is a free gift of God irrespective of what we do. Some people who pay lip service to this belief in God's initiative still act as if their true worth comes only from what they themselves do. For others salvation is a one-time event to which they can point with assurance, but which has little or no impact on the way they presently live out their lives. They do not recognize that life in Christ is not something static, but involves a relationship that is constantly to be nourished.

Is the salvation this person desires and affirms all-encompassing, or is it narrowly understood? For many people salvation means little more than deliverance from a terrible marriage, or poverty, or physical suffering. In pastoral care, then, we attempt to note what specific shape or form the desire for salvation takes in any given instance, and we evaluate it in the light of our theological understanding. Does the salvation here being sought bring freedom and well-being, or does it mean only further bondage?

6. *How adequate are this person's faith-support resources?*

Beyond the pastoral relationship, which we assume will continue, what other groups of persons and what other institutionalized traditions of help are available? To the degree that people live outside a supportive and loving community, their problems usually increase in severity.

The church has at times portrayed the family as the basic unit of spiritual nurture and support. In the case of this individual how effectively is the family providing such support? Is there an openness to other support groups—neighbors, Alcoholics Anonymous, individual or family therapy groups, the church? Is the congregation willing to provide support through individuals or fellowship groups?

A good support group is important not simply in understanding and appreciating the problem, but also in enabling the individual to build upon personal strengths and come to experience new and healthier relationships. If involved in the life of a congregation, how does this person understand and relate to "the body of Christ"? Finally, how does this person experience community, or the lack of it, through such communal events as prayer, scripture reading and study, meditation, contemplation, worship, and congregational fellowship?

7. *What sense of hope exists here?*

How does this person live with the "already now but not yet" tension of eschatological hope? In the midst of suffering, what is concretely expected of self, pastor, God?

How often we hear some prominent guest on a late-night TV talk show blandly assert: "You can do anything you want, as long as you want it badly enough and work for it hard enough!" How often we have been told that if only we pray fervently enough and have enough faith, God will grant our desires! Such notions abound in popular psychology and in popular theology as well.

But most of us recognize, when we reflect a bit, that we are *not* living the life we once envisioned. We *cannot* become anything we want, nor can we make others into just anything they, or we, want. With Paul, we often stand helpless before that "thorn in the flesh," which is uniquely our own. Eschatological hope recognizes a tension—"already now but not yet." The kingdom of God has indeed come, but it is not fully here, not yet, either for the individual or for society.[2]

Is there in the present instance, we ask, a recognition of this tension? Does that recognition produce a sense of freedom in the acceptance of limits, or does the person continue to pursue aims that are wholly beyond the realm of possibility? Has a recognition of limits led to despair? How, for example, does the gay male respond to his own sexuality and to a world that for the most part despises his sexual preference? How in his close relationships does he respond to and live with his differentness? What expectations does he place on members of the local or larger Christian and secular communities? Does he give up his vision for life, or hold onto it tenaciously in spite of realities? Is his hope based on realistic possibilities or only on "pie in the sky"?

Part and parcel of living with this tension—the "already now but not yet"—is the way one responds ethically to this world. God's love, when it comes to us, obliges us to "love the neighbor." How is the person before us responding to this obligation? Responses can run the gamut from amoral anarchy to rigid perfectionism, when persons are experiencing a broken relationship with God. On the other hand, in persons who have a sound relationship with God, there must be at least hints of a healthy sense of filial and agapic responsibility.

8. *Does freedom exist between this person and me?*

The final question brings the focus back to the pastoral relationship. Where once we asked why this person is coming to *me*, now we ask, Am I providing the greatest amount of freedom possible, or am I trying to control this person?

You think, for example, that the couple before you is not working as hard as you are to prevent their divorce. But does this judgment perhaps reflect a personal struggle to save your own troubled marriage? Does it perhaps reflect your own need to be successful as a counselor? We need to ask *ourselves*, Must I succeed, or can I allow myself to "fail"? Or even, Can my pastoral assessment be wrong?

Assessment in care, like diagnosis in medicine, is an art as well as a science. It requires education, training, and much experience. We must always be flexible, open, and ready to admit to having misinterpreted the situation. A theological template is not "etched in stone." The assessing must be attentive, cautious, and continually up for review.

Finally, in this regard, we ask, Am I open to allowing this parishioner to minister to me? The question does not imply confusion about who is pastor and who is asking for help, but it does mean acknowledging that in the course of our ministering we actually receive as well as give. The ministry we have received from God includes the privilege of receiving another person's trust. And in the faces that look trustfully toward us for help, we experience the face of God. Within the very pain and suffering that comes our way God comes to us too.

Pastoral Assessment in Practice

These eight questions model a method of pastoral assessment that may be worth trying. A concrete case can illustrate its practicability and keep it from being merely an intellectual exercise. It may even point up the nature and usefulness of the theological template in pastoral care.

The telephone rang at the quiet home of Paul Williams on a Sunday afternoon in late October, just as the pastor was settling down in a comfortable sofa to watch his favorite team on TV. A distraught male voice at the other end asked to see the pastor as soon as possible. The problem was described only as "a real emergency." Paul agreed to meet the man at the church office in thirty minutes.

When he arrived the pastor was met by the distraught man, who was accompanied by his wife. Neither Gerald nor Jennie were members of the congregation; they had been referred by a member who was their neighbor. Gerald was a Caucasian, possibly in his late thirties, middle-class in appearance. Jennie, also Caucasian, appeared to be in her mid-thirties, attractive, and well-dressed. Gerald had a distended abdomen, a sickly pale complexion, and seemed physically shaken. His voice trembled as he spoke and he was on the verge of tears. Jennie was composed and soft-spoken, but the picture of fatigue.

When Pastor Williams asked, "How can I be of help?" Jennie told of her decision to end their twelve-year marriage. She spoke of Gerald's drinking problem over ten of the past twelve years and indicated that her husband was unwilling to admit his alcoholism and his need of help. She concluded by repeating her firm decision to divorce him, "I cannot live a life of watching him drink himself to death." When Pastor Williams asked why she had accompanied her husband here to the office, she acknowledged her desire to be supportive in Gerald's efforts at getting help for himself.

Gerald tearfully responded to the pastor's question, this time addressed to him, by admitting his drinking problem and saying he realized he was losing what he cherished most in life—his wife. He further admitted his desire for help, but made a strong appeal for Jennie to give him another chance. He begged her forgiveness and explicitly reminded her of Jesus' teaching on the need to forgive a person who was truly sorry.

As the conversation continued, Pastor Williams learned that this couple had no children and very few friends; their respective sets of parents lived at opposite ends of the state. Both husband and wife were employed, apparently experiencing successful work relationships. There appeared to be no evidence of Gerald's drinking having yet interfered with his work.

In summary, their problem was verbalized in two ways. The wife's position was: "I am divorcing him, but I care enough to want him to get help." The husband's position was: "I have a drinking problem and I want help; but I also want her to stay and give me another chance."

Pastoral assessment began with the first meeting and involved immediate use of a theological template. Paul reflected on question one in order to understand the expectations these people had brought with them to the pastor's office.

Initially, at least, it appeared that Jennie regarded the pastor not as a reconciler, but as one through whom her husband might be able to get help for his alcoholism. The couple had had no prior acquaintance with Pastor Williams. Perhaps they sought him out because their neighbor had characterized him as an understanding and helpful person. Jennie clearly assumed that a pastor would have ties with other relevant helpers in the community.

Gerald, on the other hand, did not see the pastor primarily as a means of attaining further help with his alcoholism. He responded instead to the image of the pastor as "moral teacher," as potential leverage for persuading his wife not to leave him. In effect, Gerald was saying to his wife, "The pastor will agree with me that you should forgive me." He may also have had some awareness that his (and their) problems were bigger than he could handle and that he needed divine assistance.

Pastor Williams regarded Jennie's expectations as the more realistic of the two. He wondered if Gerald's expectations might be indicative of a style of manipulative relating, although he could not of course dismiss altogether the ethical question raised by the husband.

In this first encounter question two, about God, found little in the way of direct expression. Brief reference was made to Jesus, implying the authority of Jesus' teachings, but only in the context of Gerald's effort to convince Jennie that she was wrong to choose a divorce. What or who was the husband's God? What determines Gerald's decision making? Tentatively one might answer that Gerald's god was nothing but an idol—the bottle, or whatever the bottle offered him. Gerald's claim that his most cherished relationship was that with his wife seemed to be contradicted by his actual history. Jennie's understanding of God did not become at all apparent in this initial visit.

Question three asks about the role of sin. Gerald's drinking problem and manipulativeness revealed a person who had placed himself at the center of his own existence. His past choices had resulted in the actual destruction of his marriage and the potential destruction of his own body. Guilt was perceived not so much in Gerald's asking his wife's forgiveness as in Jennie's comment that he had been drinking himself to death. What guilt would cause him to inflict such a severe self-punishment? By not taking Gerald at his word the moment he asked for forgiveness, the pastor was demonstrating his own assessment that repentance was not yet at hand.

Pastor Williams felt that the topics of faith and salvation raised in questions four and five had not yet been broached, at least as far as the husband was concerned, What was Gerald's capacity for faith? What was his conception of salvation? Had he in fact drunk himself into oblivion? As regards the wife, the pastor thought he saw some signs of faith; she trusted others to help a person she could no longer help. She may even have been trusting her husband, feeling perhaps for the first time that he was about to choose life over death. She saw her salvation at this time primarily as deliverance from the daily exposure to her husband's slow suicide. As with most people in crisis, Jennie was having difficulty seeing beyond immediate relief to larger personal needs.

With respect to question six the pastor had deep concerns. Both persons seemed isolated from any recognizable faith support-group; they were not a part of the fellowship of believers. Besides himself there were apparently only a few nameless and not very close relationships at work that could conceivably constitute any kind of support network.

Question seven, about living within the "already now but not yet" tension, was difficult to answer because neither person showed any clear sense of direction—except for Jennie's wanting to get out! Yet even in her the pastor did not detect despair. She seemed to be accepting her finitude realistically, recognizing that after she had done all she could to help change her husband she now had to abandon him to others. Gerald was still testing his finitude, refusing to recognize limits; there was no clear recognition of God as the provider of all strength and succor for the future, only a slight hint of some movement in this direction signaled by the fact of his going to a minister.

Question eight is as important as question one. How did Pastor Williams feel about these persons? He did not like being pulled away from the football game. Had anger over losing his personal time perhaps diminished his ability to listen? Had it caused him to be condemning in his judgments? Did the prominence of the drinking problem trigger his apparent sympathy with the wife? Was she viewed in a morally superior light as the long-suffering wife simply because the interview had not produced much data about her as a person? Was the pastor's hope for these persons and for their marriage tainted by his frustrations over the long years of marriage counseling with couples who always opted anyway for divorce?

These then were some of the initial queries with which Pastor Williams began his assessment process. They helped him focus and apply a theological template in his pastoral care. On the basis of such a theological assessment he would develop a response that might include a whole range of possibilities: continuing pastoral relationship, medical examination, decision counseling, Alcoholics Anonymous and Alanon, involvement with a church fellowship, theological confrontation, spiritual guidance, marriage counseling. His systematic reflection helped the pastor develop a much broader and deeper understanding of Gerald and Jennie than might otherwise have been possible. If his relationship with them did in fact continue, as it was expected to do, Pastor Williams' assessment would of course undergo repeated refinement through continuing use of his theological template.

As pastoral care returns to its roots, it will rediscover the significance of its own theological perspective as a primary frame of reference—as a template for correlating with the specific personal situations encountered in pastoral care. The template here suggested is, of course, only one such framework, but it is offered in the hope that it may prove helpful as a methodological aid for pastors in the self-conscious formulation of their own theological templates.

The acknowledgment and active use of the theological template in pastoral assessment will be a key component in our much-needed correlation of theology and pastoral care.

NOTES

1. Paul Pruyser, *The Minister as Diagnostician* (Philadelphia: Westminster Press, 1976).

2. Alastair Campbell, *Rediscovering Pastoral Care* (London: Darton, Longman, & Todd, 1981), p. 35.

3. The Word of God

Protestants today, as part of their legacy from the Reformation, still think of ministry as essentially proclamation of the word and administration of the sacraments. Unfortunately in too many instances this notion of a ministry of word and sacraments has had little influence on current pastoral care theory and practice. In fact, pastoral care in our time has had difficulty in recognizing any relationship whatsoever to ministry itself, and particularly to a ministry of word and sacraments. Fancy verbal footwork has often been required to portray pastoral care as being any more central to the task of ministry than, say, the coaching of a basketball team in the church gymnasium.

The development of nondirective counseling may have contributed to this situation, helping push pastoral care to the fringes of ministry. Developed in the forties and fifties under Carl Rogers, this modern psychotherapeutic model breathed fresh life into a practice that had come to be steeped in an outmoded tradition. The earlier traditional methods of pastoral care had been creating increasing discomfort among its practitioners. Pastors had begun to recognize that their parishioners were no longer satisfied with facile answers, even if taken directly from the Bible—answers that did not take seriously the concrete realities of today's human situations. As attitudes toward authority in general began to change, people also grew less willing to accept at face value the authoritative solutions offered by their pastor, an authority who often did not listen carefully to their cries of pain or try to understand the real issues they were confronting and who certainly was not integral to any specific solution of their problems. It was through the newer nondirective counseling methods that pastors began to learn contemporary skills of authentic listening and of establishing rapport. Drawing upon psychology and counseling to further their ability to care, pastors who had been trained in the older methodologies now began to find increasing opportunities for intervening helpfully in the lives of their parishioners. The newer nondirective model proved as popular as it was beneficial. Because it relied so heavily on eductive guidance, however, eliciting from people's own lives and values the criteria for decision making, pastors who were drawn to it also lost to some degree their ministerial identity.[1]

Now the essence of pastoral care, as of all ministry sharing in the legacy of the Reformation, is the proclamation or communication of the word—that word which became flesh, lived among us, and died reconciling us with God. Care-giving that is truly pastoral proclaims this message. It is therefore not something on the fringes of ministry but at its very center.

The Word of God

What is the word of God? An understanding of "word" in biblical parlance involves several considerations.[2]

In the Old Testament, Israel made little or no distinction between a word itself and the thing or event implied by that word. *Dabar* (word) could represent an event in history or nature as well as a spoken or written word. When in the creation story God spoke, the world was created: "By the word of the Lord the heavens were made" (Ps. 33:6). The word was God's way of acting! The word was also the typical way by which God's will was made known and providential guidance offered to the world. "Word of the Lord" is an expression used to denote a medium of revelation: Yahweh speaks (e.g., "the word of the Lord that came to . . .") and the prophet hears.

In the New Testament "the word" (usually *logos*) takes on additional connotations. James Sanders points to six basic usages: the Old Testament law (e.g., Mark 7:13); a particular Old Testament passage (John 10:35); God's revealed will (Luke 11:28); the word proclaimed by Jesus (Luke 5:1); the Christian message (Luke 8:11); and the incarnate Christ (John 1:1-14). In this last passage "word" is used as a title for Christ himself.[3]

Even a brief review of these biblical understandings of "the word" helps not only to clarify the concept but also to provide the basis for viewing pastoral care in terms of the word. Pastoral care involves both proclamation (or communication) of the word and a mutual listening for it and speaking it. Our cursory reflection on the meanings of *dabar* and *logos* suggests four key considerations: the word is God's revelation to humanity, it establishes and extends relationship, it is the mode of communication of the faith, and it is expressed both verbally (as spoken or written) and visibly (as act).[4]

God's Revelation to Humanity

As the communication of God's will to us, the word is the incarnation of the Totally Other in our midst. To quote Edward Schillebeeckx, "In and through his historically conditioned humanity, Christ is the revelation of God in our midst. Thus He is the word of God: God Himself, the Son, speaking personally to man in the man Jesus. A fellow man, who treats us person-to-person, is personally God, the Son. Each truly human act of Christ is therefore a word of God directed toward mankind, more strongly so than the Old Testament history of salvation."[5] C. K. Barrett's commentary on John notes that both in the church and in philosophy *logos* was a common term describing a process of self-expression.[6] In this sense the word is God's ongoing self-communication, God's revelation or reaching out to humanity. It is the

communication that takes place in the God-human relationship. It is the word of promise, the promise of redemption.
Finally, it is the proclamation that God will forgive our sin, not
because we are deserving, but because God is the loving and
merciful One who cares for us and desires our fellowship.

Gerhard Ebeling, in summarizing the biblical witness,
points out:

Word of God, according to the biblical tradition, thus seeks to be
understood as a word event that does not go out of date but constantly
renews itself, does not create closed areas of special interest but opens
up the world, does not enforce uniformity but is linguistically creative.
Of course it is startling—but only because it reveals what was hidden.
Certainly it is tradition, yet tradition of a kind that sets us free for our
own present. Whatever is put forth as word of God is certainly
changed into an antiquated, constricting word that enslaves us, and
thus becomes the opposite of what the word of God is, whenever it is
denied responsible participation in the word event.[7]

The word is thus a living proclamation that occurs in a
specific situation. It is not an abstract philosophical concept,
a pseudonym for "reason." It is not an impersonal force in
the universe. The word is One who shows personal interest
in us—who establishes a relationship with us. As Rudolph
Bultmann has said, "If we return to the real significance of
'word,' implying as it does a relationship between speaker
and hearer, then the word can become an event to the hearer,
because it brings him into this relationship."[8]

Establishing and Extending Relationship

God addresses us in the word; in the word we encounter
the One who is indeed with us. This meeting of God and
person in the word has about it a sense of call—the call into
relationship. The word is still God, but God as word shows
an intense interest in each of us. The emphasis is not on a
passive word—not marks on parchment—but on a living,
active, vital occurrence. The word enters our lives as a
creative force, motivating, prompting, and enlivening us.

Through it we are brought into God's presence; we come to stand, as the Reformers put it, *coram deo*.

As in an intimate relationship deep feelings, secrets, hopes, and wishes are shared, so in the word God is revealed to us. Thus revelation is not only general (as in nature) or specific (as in written scriptures) but also intensely personal, tailored for each of us. The word specifically addresses every individual as individual—as a person possessed of personality, intuition, likes, dislikes, woes, and joys.

God's revelation addresses us in human form—through other people, art, drama, literature, our own thoughts and visions. Whenever God speaks to us there is a new incarnation of the word—one that is directed to us in, through, and by a human word. This word is God in personal relationship, and the message it brings is an intimate, personalized revelation.

Because of the character of word as incarnational address to the people of God, every human experience is potentially revelatory. No boundaries of denomination, dogma, or religious practice determine God's self-revelation through the word. Neither do race, class, social standing, I.Q., educational level, gender, mental health or emotional stability, disposition or temperament, cleanliness, or perfect pitch. God's word can encounter us at any place, in any hour, through any event.

This is why we must listen. We must be prepared to hear the word in any and every circumstance. The Christian who is obsessed with doing, even the doing of honest and upright things, and has little time either for quiet reflection and meditation or for genuine engagement with others runs the risk of trampling the word and missing what God has to say.

Communication of the Faith

Every communication of the gospel involves an appearance of the word embodied in human form. The term *communication* has two basic meanings: (1) it can refer to the passing along of information, as in a help-wanted ad listing the types of employment available at the opening of a new industrial plant; (2) communication can also be understood as personal sharing, including emotional elements as well as intellectual content.

In effect, what distinguishes these two types of communication is commonly conveyed in the prepositional distinction between *about* and *of*. The first type—passing along information—is verbal; whether written or spoken, it involves the conveying of data *about* something that may or may not be useful to the listener or reader for *knowing*. With the second type—personal sharing—a relationship is established or extended; a part *of* oneself is offered in such a way that the stuff imparted is available for *experiencing*. In the case of the former, the speaker-listener relationship is strictly "business" (in Martin Buber's terms, an I-It relationship), with the listener being merely an "object" or observer. In the case of the latter, true encounter occurs between speaker and listener (an I-Thou relationship), and attending concern and compassion are expressed.

Dissociating the two modes of communication may not be altogether helpful, or even possible. For example, an advertisement for a job may communicate more to me than just information about an available position; it may create within me excitement, hope, anticipation of a new possibility. Likewise in the sharing of a personal encounter, facts germane to the relationship in process may also be transmitted. In both instances the communication has an impact on the listener—the person is somehow altered because of what happens.

In communication of the faith, what happens is an encounter with God the word. It is a message not merely *about* the word but *of* the word:

When faith and God are put together, we may put it thus: we are not concerned just with a piece of information about God, but with participation in him, that is, with an event in which God himself is communicated. If what I have already briefly said is right, then such a communication would be a true meeting with God, and it would not be in the least preposterous, but perfectly appropriate, that this meeting with God should take place in the word as an event.

Of course, it is not any and every word about God that is a communication of faith, that is, that can communicate the faith which is a participation in God himself. To use the language of the biblical tradition, it is the Word of God alone which can do this.[9]

A word is never merely a "word"; it is also an expression of one's self in relation to another. The power of the word is the power of *being* itself; it embraces emotion, is relational, and addresses our past, present, and future. The followers of Jesus transmitted the word of Christ; they "went about preaching the word" (Acts 8:4). It was not *a* word *about* Christ but indeed *the* word that God was embodied *in* Christ.

The Verbal and Visible Word

Communication is both verbal and nonverbal. Gestures as well as words portray meaning. A gentle touch can tell more than a thousand words; a look can communicate an indescribable feeling. Crucial ideas can be made explicit by a gesture, deep meanings by an image. Likewise God's word is both verbally articulated and visually presented to us. Robert Jenson makes the point:

The word in which God—for the present, *any* God—communicates himself must be an embodied word, a word "with" some visible reality, a grant of divine objectivity. We must be able to see and touch what we are to apprehend from God. . . . A disembodied, purely linguistic communication, however it might occur and whoever or whatever might be able so to speak, could not reveal God. God's presence must grant an object.[10]

Revelation occurs as the word is embodied. God reveals God's self (as in Christ) in both spoken and visible form.

"The word comes to the element; and so there is a sacrament, that is, a sort of visible word."[11] Augustine's famous sacramental phrase has been interpreted and reinterpreted throughout the centuries. Although understandings of "the visible word" have varied, one major theme has remained constant: when God speaks to us, the word comes through some element, some form of visible reality. In terms of the sacrament the word of God is the wafer broken, or the water gently sprinkled. Augustine seems to suggest that liturgies and rites gain their efficacy from the word, from God's communication with God's people. The elements in the sacrament are God's way of securing the word in our sensory world and thus making it accessible to us.

Although Augustine and most of his early interpreters contrasted visible word and invisible word, the Reformers shifted the emphasis. They contrasted the visible with the verbal, spoken, or audible word, focusing on the distinction between hearing and the other senses. Augustine was reinterpreted to say that God speaks to us not only in language symbols but also in those images and signs that are seen, touched, tasted, smelled, and grasped—by any of the senses. This Reformation distinction between the verbal and the sensory ultimately can assist us in our clarification of the meaning of pastoral care as communication of the word, because in every instance of effective communication some of the things transmitted are put in the form of sentences (the verbal word) and some are relayed to the senses in other ways—through gestures, imagery, tones, tactile impression (the visible word).

"The verbal word," of course, includes more than simply the preaching of the word; it encompasses also teaching, scripture reading, and the written or spoken sharing of the gospel. Similarly "the visible word" includes more than simply administration of the sacraments; its meaning can be extended even to such things as an icon, Brahms' *Requiem*, a jazz mass, an embrace, time freely given to listen to another, a warm smile, a covered dish meal brought to the recently bereaved, one's ministry of presence, the sign of the cross. These too are all crucial ways in which God comes to us. The supreme instance of the visible word, of course, is the incarnation of Christ.

God is the Holy Other, inaccessible to us; it is through the incarnation of the word in gestures, rites, and other elements of the sensory sphere that the hidden is revealed and the truth is spoken visibly, in ways that we can apprehend. To quote Jenson, "The Father knows himself in Jesus' body that walked to the cross, and in the objects that are used and used up in the gospel-communication. That is, he knows them as visible *words*."[12] Or, from Luther: "God . . . sets before us no word or commandment without including with it something material and outward, and proffering it to us. To Abraham he gave the word including with it his son Isaac [Gen. 15:4 ff.]. To Saul he gave the word including with it the slaying of the Amalekites [I Sam. 15:2 ff.]. To Noah he gave the word including with it the rainbow [Gen. 9:8 ff.]. And so on. You find no word of God in the entire Scriptures in which something material and outward is not contained and presented."[13]

The church generally, and especially the Protestant church since the Reformation, is most familiar with the verbal word. In fact, in churches that are accustomed to less formal services, the sermon has so moved to the fore that worship has become almost entirely a hearing of the audible articulation of the gospel. Although ministry usually has been understood, even in such churches, as a matter of proclaiming (or preaching) the word and administering the sacraments, the sacraments are often little more than an appendage to the audible word.

God, however, is really present in both the verbal word and the visible word. The sacraments are not just *signs* derived from God; God is truly there. The sermon is patently not just words *about* God but the word *of* God. A pastor's empathy for the parents of a dying child is not just a sign of God's love; God has promised to be there. God's desire is to communicate with God's people. As Schillebeeckx has noted, "The whole world of creatures became a 'gratia externa,' an exteriorizing of grace, that is, grace itself in visible operation. Within this world-embracing manifestation of the Lord, the ministry of the word and the rituals of the sacraments are only the glowing focus of the visible presence of grace."[14]

Words or phrases about God can say what they mean only as they are embodied, only as they become a "visible presence of grace"; for it is only as they are acted out and apprehended that they become the word of God. The often trite and offhand "God loves you" can become truly alive and meaningful to a person when it is the response offered by a minister who has listened and graciously received and shared the turmoil bound up inside that person's being—then the word has indeed become flesh and dwells among us.

Pastoral Care as Communication of the Word

The Primacy of the Word

Hans Asmussen in his 1934 work *Die Seelsorge* described pastoral care as "proclamation of the word of God . . . the message is told to the individual face to face."[15] More recently Paul Tillich said much the same thing: "If we assume the rightful claim of the ministry to be that the minister pronounces, preaches, teaches, and in counseling mediates the 'word of God,' no question can arise about the relevance of his ministry for every human being."[16] The German theologian Eduard Thurneysen agrees: "Proclamation of the word is therefore the beginning and end of all true pastoral care. . . . Pastoral care exists in the church as the communication of the word of God to individuals. Like every legitimate function of the church, pastoral care springs from the living word of God given to the church. This word demands to be communicated in various ways."[17] Although they might vary in their understandings of what constitutes the word, Asmussen, Thurneysen, and Tillich are at one in pointing to the communication of God's word as the purpose of pastoral care and counseling.

The Reformers emphasized the primacy of the word of God in all ministry. For them the word is more than just an audible message preached during worship. In his treatise *On the Councils and the Church* Luther asserts, "Now, wherever you hear or see this word preached, believed, professed, and lived, do not doubt that the true *ecclesia sancta catholica*, 'a Christian holy people,' must be there."[18] Ministry, and indeed the church, exists whenever and wherever the verbal or visible word is proclaimed. Luther performed pastoral care along with all other tasks of ministry, including his teaching duties, without dissociating such ministry from his service of the word.[19] He believed that all ministry arises out of and returns to the word.

Of course, when the sermon is preached or the liturgy intoned, the minister's service is of necessity formal in nature. It cannot be tailored to one specific person or family in the manner of pastoral care. While care and counseling allow for a more private, individualized mode of proclamation, they still retain the fundamental character of proclamation—communication of the word.

Even care that is addressed to the most isolated and specific of human concerns must be seen as having its relationship to God's word. Such care involves listening deeply to these concerns, but always in the light of the word. Thurneysen illustrates this point: "Pastoral care is a conversation resting on a very definite assumption. It intends to be a conversation that proceeds from the word of God and leads to the word of God. . . . At first, they [the two persons involved in pastoral care conversation] perhaps do not mention this word of God and its content at all; instead they speak of certain very concrete problems and concerns of their lives. Even so they proceed on the assumption that the word of God whereby they are addressed or are to be addressed is important for these very problems and concerns."[20]

If pastoral care is indeed the communication of the word, then it must also be done in a hermeneutically responsible way. Instead of interpreting the word while poring over scripture, commentaries, and theological handbooks, however, the minister accomplishes the hermeneutical task while concretely listening to others pour out their distress. Pastors practice a kind of "trenches hermeneutic." They lack the luxury of being able to lean back in a chair and cogitate on what they have been reading. Instead they must listen *to* the person and *for* the word simultaneously and structure their care in response to the event of the word. It was pointed out at the end of the previous chapter that in concrete care situations the correlation of theology and pastoral care frequently happens almost automatically. Indeed, pastors rely on their prior theological reflection—listening to the word—to shape their present response to the other person.

This task of interpreting God's word cannot be bypassed in the name of providing concrete, issue-oriented counsel. Psychological counseling, of course, can greatly enhance the quality of the care being offered to specific persons, even in the midst of the mutual listening for the word. But it can also easily supplant the hermeneutical task of the minister so that God's word is not heard at all and pastoral care deteriorates from proclamation into social work. Beneficial as it may be, social work is not pastoral care; its purpose is rather different. The purpose of pastoral care is to listen to and speak the word.

Two Modes of the Word

The word, we have said, is the communication of God which, addressing us both verbally and visibly, establishes relationships. Verbally the word is transmitted through preaching, teaching, and the scriptures; visibly the word comes through the sacrament, acts of kindness, and the ministry of presence.

Pastoral care must be alert to this twofold mode of address. In actual practice it has often ignored one of these two manifestations of the word. Traditional pastoral care, with its emphasis on inductive guidance and urging the cared-for to adopt *a priori* values as the basis for decision making,[21] tended to elevate the speaking of the word at the expense of listening deeply to a person's own pain or distress. A legacy from the nineteenth century, it did not take seriously the learnings from contemporary psychology, but instead used as key resources the scriptures, occasional services, and prayer. It frequently consisted of the pastor telling parishioners, ostensibly on the basis of scripture, what they must do. In effect, it was conversational preaching tailored to the pastor's view of the parishioner's problem. Indeed it might be said that traditional pastoral care strongly emphasized the verbal word in a ministry of speaking, while often ignoring the visible word.

The nondirective approach of Carl Rogers, coming as a welcome reaction to this traditional care, helped pastors listen more carefully and establish a solid relationship of rapport. It took more seriously the learnings of modern psychology. The pastor became less of a distant parent figure and more of an emotionally close friend. This warm confidante, at once friend and pastor, changed pastoral care from a ministry of speaking the word through scripture and prayer to a ministry of compassion. A verbal word addressing such matters as sin, justification by grace, and God's intervention in our lives, however, was rarely spoken. Indeed it might be said that nondirective pastoral care strongly emphasized the visible word in a ministry of presence, while often ignoring the verbal word.

Charles Gerkin has characterized the dilemma common to pastors caught between the traditional and the nondirective approaches:

Faced with persons suffering the double crisis of chaotic experience and muddled faith, the pastor may well be tempted in two opposite directions both leading toward pastoral identity crisis. Speaking the right words that no longer evoke the expected response becomes a vacuous exercise that leads to the despair of having been rendered impotent. On the other hand, there is the temptation so to identify with the bewilderment and confusion of the doubting victim of crisis that the pastor becomes a victim of that doubt that renders ministry an apology. Somewhere between these two extremes of verbally faithful ministry that fails to communicate, and debilitating doubt that forsakes the pastoral task, the Christian pastor must find his or her integrity.[22]

While it is easy to be swayed in either one of these two directions, it is difficult but most essential to find that elusive middle between the extremes. Recalling that the word is communicated both verbally and visibly may be the key to a restoration of integrity to pastoral ministry. Indeed pastoral care that is faithful to the word of God attends to both the verbal word and the visible word. God communicates to and establishes relationship with people in both these ways, verbally and visibly. Pastoral care that emphasizes only one mode of the word is less than faithful to God's own manner of communication. We need the pastoral care that incorporates both modes of address. Sometimes a hug, an attending glance, or a listening ear will be just right; at other times a verbal articulation of God's love in Christ will give impact to the word.

People exercise considerable discrimination when it comes to choosing the person with whom they will share their burdens. Hurting people do not come to their minister primarily because the pastor is available and pastoral service is cheap; they do not come only for a listening ear or a fresh affirmation of their personhood. Many come precisely because the pastor symbolizes that Other who, they sense, can somehow help inject meaning into their struggles. If then we neglect to speak to them of God, offering only uncritical warmth and affirmation, we give the people a stone rather than the Bread of Life; instead of providing eternal nourishment we simply nurture good feelings for the short term. Where issues of sin, guilt, and reconciliation in Christ are at the root of the matter, we may be proffering nothing but psychological techniques, good though these may be. We must be alert to—caught up in the ministry of—imparting the verbal word.

Ministers, of course, can easily be too quick with words, too ready with facile solutions. We need to appreciate the power of the visible word. Bonhoeffer says it well:

Let us ask why it is that precisely in thoroughly grave situations, for instance when I am with someone who has suffered a bereavement, I often decide to adopt a "penultimate" attitude . . . remaining silent as a sign that I share in the bereaved man's helplessness in the face of such a grievous event, and not speaking the biblical words of comfort which are, in fact, known to me and available to me. Why am I often unable to open my mouth, when I ought to give expression to the ultimate? And why, instead, do I decide on an expression of thoroughly penultimate human solidarity? Is it from mistrust of the power of the ultimate word? Is it from fear of men? Or is there some good positive reason for such an attitude, namely, that my knowledge of the word, my having it at my finger-tips, in other words my being, so to speak, spiritually master of the situation, bears only the appearance of the ultimate, but is in reality itself something entirely penultimate? Does one not in some cases, by remaining deliberately in the penultimate, perhaps point all the more genuinely to the ultimate, which God will speak in His own time?[23]

And in such situations the visual word can sometimes verify (or refute) the spoken word.

In pastoral care we stand between the word and the deeply troubled person. The carer has the potential, as Tillich put it, to "mediate" God's word to this other individual. The situation is much like that which we experience at a ballet. The dancers by their physical movement express emotion and narrate the story, while the libretto with its text helps clarify and augment these movements, actually enhancing the visual impression. But each needs the other. The movements without the libretto or the libretto without the movements would reduce the total impact that might otherwise be had from both verbally reading what the dance is about and at the same time visually seeing it in all its raw emotion. The total experience comes from a proper blending of the two. In pastoral care the dancer's movements may transmit God's love, but the libretto clarifies it and gives it a name—Christ.

The Sovereignty of the Word

What is not a part of our understanding, as Bonhoeffer suggests, what we can never know in any given pastoral care situation, is precisely when a penultimate word, whether verbal or visible, may become ultimate. Whether ours is a word or a gesture, a recitation of John 3:16 or a spontaneous embrace, a verbal sharing of the transformation made in my life by Christ's presence, or a period of quiet empathetic listening—any one or more of these events can become the ultimate word. Each is potentially transforming. Each can mean the changing of human articulations or gesticulations into the word of God. The frail, finite presence of the pastor can become a window through which the person in pain catches a glimpse of the infinite.

From the general discussion to this point it might perhaps seem as if God's word would come naturally and automatically to the troubled person through the use of proper care and counseling techniques involving both verbal and visible expressions. That impression is quite false. The serious danger in such a view lies in the assumption that it is we ministers who cause the word to come. As pastoral carers we are right if we see ourselves as bearers of Christ to other people, but wrong if we assume that we are that because of what we do. Carers who hold such a notion have lost sight of the *pneuma* that blows where it wishes and is not controlled by our actions (John 3:8). The word of God is uncontrollable; we can neither manipulate it nor force it. Faith comes only through the work of the Holy Spirit. Only as the word of God claims the mannerisms and formulations of our sermon, or the gestures and phrases of our pastoral act, do they become word—what Bonhoeffer called ultimate.

For Luther, "All that our body does outwardly and physically, if God's Word is added to it and it is done through faith, is in reality and in name done spiritually."[24] Our care becomes spiritual care only when the alien word transforms it. As God's co-workers (I Cor. 3:1-9) we reach out and admonish other persons (II Cor. 5:20), not as if all is dependent on us but rather with gentleness, sincerity, and tenderness, waiting for the One who both wills and does (Phil. 2:13).

John Cobb says it well: "Pastors above all will know that they are at most midwives of God's grace."[25] And the people we serve will know that neither the awareness of sin nor the certainty of forgiveness and reconciliation comes from us; both are awakened—in the pastoral carer as well as in the parishioner—solely by God's word through the moving of the Spirit. Thus the word is communicated not *by* the pastor, but *through* the pastor as the Spirit transforms the pastoral care encounter.

Listening for and Speaking the Word

Mutual Listening for the Word

"So faith comes from what is heard" (Rom. 10:17; cf. Gal. 3:2, 5). Paul repeatedly asserts that the hearing of the word precedes faith. Luther reiterates Paul's stress on hearing: "If you want to obtain grace, then see to it that you hear the word of God attentively or meditate on it diligently. The word, I say, and only the word, is the vehicle of God's grace."[26]

In so many ways contemporary society places humans at the center of the universe, assuring us that whatever we have or are is determined by what we ourselves do. It is only natural for us, then, in matters of faith, to assume that here too we can always attain our own righteousness, our own justification. This self-centered belief can be changed in only one way—by the hearing and accepting of the word of God. For the word declares firmly and clearly that our justification, in fact whatever good we do, is wholly the result of an alien word. It is only as we are addressed from the outside that we are reconciled; it is only as we listen that we can begin to understand God's will for us and be declared righteous.

Pastoral care involves listening for the word of God. It does not lightly assume that it has authoritative control of the word. It recognizes, as Luther pointed out, that every Christian must daily "creep unto your baptism."[27] The carer's task is not merely to proclaim the word to the parishioner; carer and cared-for alike—both being frail, fragile, and sinful creatures—must mutually and humbly await the address of the word.

This waiting for the word does not mean that pastoral care is purely passive. It does not mean that we cannot use the best available psychological methods, although at times we will eschew them. It does not mean that we can avoid the responsibility of preparing ourselves to be the best pastoral carers we can possibly be, although at times it seems that much of our training is for naught. It does not mean that we should not carefully and keenly listen to the other, for what comes to us in and through the other's utterances often is God's word.

Our mutual waiting for the word does mean that we cannot predict God's address. It does mean that God may sometimes choose the pain of another as a vehicle through which to share a message with me. It does mean that as two of us speak in the pastoral care event, as two of us listen to each other, we also listen attentively in order to hear the word.

This waiting for the word's address can well change aspects of the care being offered today. Our care need not be so frenzied, so doing-oriented, so worried. Though as pastors we do everything we can to care for the other person, ultimate care comes as a gift from the outside—as an alien word that finds us when and where it will. Faith involves the assurance that God's word *will* come, but not the knowledge of when or how. As Thurneysen puts it, "Listening to our neighbor, we shall at the same time listen to the word of God and seek to perceive its answer to our neighbor's problem."[28]

Speaking the Word

"When Christians live together the time must inevitably come when in some crisis one person will have to declare God's word and will to another. . . . Nothing can be more cruel than the tenderness that consigns another to his sin. Nothing can be more compassionate than the severe rebuke that calls a brother back from the path of sin."[29] In pastoral care we wait for the Spirit's address, which meets us in both the visible and the verbal. But, as Bonhoeffer has so eloquently stated, there is a time in the care we offer others when a verbal word must be spoken, when we must attempt to speak the word of God to those others—be it a word of judgment or of grace. To be silent, to withhold this word in the name of compassion, would be cruel—a departure from the proclamatory task of pastoral care.

To construe pastoral care in terms of proclamation is not to ignore the difficulty of the task of speaking about God today. Indeed, as we noted in the "Introduction" it may be easier in our time and culture to talk to others about such taboo subjects as sex than it is to speak to them about faith in Christ. If pastoral care is supposed to involve the speaking of God's word, then it has an onerous and challenging task. Perhaps this is why pastoral care, being obliged to speak of God in a "post–Christian" culture, has tended to fall into one of two camps—communicating either the verbal at the expense of the visible or the visible at the expense of the verbal.

Practitioners of traditional pastoral care speak *about* God but frequently fail to establish rapport with the person to whom they speak; in their stress on the verbal they neglect the visible word, forgetting that God communicates to us not mechanically but within the framework of an intimate relationship. On the other hand, practitioners of the nondirective approach, aware that God's word is incarnate in a relationship, forget that God not only *shows* God's word, God also secures it *verbally*. Out of deference for the person to whom they speak and for the delicacy of a communication that cannot be forced, they lose the ability to speak about God at all and, distrusting the power of the verbal word about God, they often say nothing. Gerhard Ebeling pinpoints our exacting task in speaking of God today:

We must not irresponsibly continue to talk of God, nor irresponsibly stop doing so. Yet to a disquieting extent both things are happening today. And both are poisonous, albeit in different ways. . . .

Now, however, we find ourselves in an age in which responsible talk of God has to satisfy extreme demands. Never before was there so great a gulf between the linguistic tradition of the Bible and the language that is actually spoken. Hence, never before was it so easy to suspect that God is merely a matter of tradition. Never before was the task of answering for God in our word put before us so radically. The problem today, seen as a whole, is indeed not that there is any lack of institutions and publications which provide possibilities for speaking of God. On the contrary, the problem is how a genuine word of God is to be asserted in the midst of this tremendous inflation of existing possibilities.[30]

Ebeling goes on to describe most contemporary God-talk as "ghetto language."[31] Although superficial talk of God is everywhere, the languages of academia, business, and science have become so technical that talk about God seems strangely out of place in those milieus. Thus, apart from some occasional vague reference, language about God is reserved for Sunday worship, Christian education, baptism, marriage (maybe), funerals, and certain religious or "devotional" writing. "Talk of God occupies only one narrow sector, and is itself in turn split into many dialects. . . . Outside of the appointed reserves it is extraordinarily difficult even in intimate circles to use the word 'God' at all."[32]

Granted, there is this global dissipation of God-talk in our time. It is nonetheless essential that even today we speak the word of God in pastoral care. In asserting this I do not mean to minimize the problem. Merely updating the language, for example, or reformulating it in alluring jargon, surely will not suffice. Although the systematic removal of "thee" and "thou" may help, and the recasting of our images and metaphors from those of an agrarian society into those of a city culture may serve a valid purpose, such attempts can also belie an uneasiness about the real task—indeed a lack of confidence in God and the word—that may be at the heart of our present difficulty. To recast the word in modern terms, or heroically attempt to proclaim it in spite of all odds, may be to forget that the power of the word is from God and not from what we do to parse it, adorn it, disguise it, or even improve it. Ebeling puts it this way: "Our own age has largely lost the courage—many even believe it has altogether forfeited the possibility—to speak of God."[33]

The courage to proclaim comes not from our own dauntless attempts to "speak it anyway" or disguise it in modern lingo; it arises from the daily nourishment of our own relationship to God within the community of faith. What is needed in pastoral care today is a new and different kind of listening to the word's address if in our acts of care we are to proclaim the word courageously.

Could it be that twentieth-century Protestant pastoring, in its frenzy to meet other people's needs, has so invested itself in *doing* as to neglect its prior responsibility of *listening* to the word? In a technological society with its emphasis on human capacity to alter anything and everything—the environment, government, economy, genes, other people—is it possible that pastoral ministry has tried to manipulate the word too, and in so doing lost faith in the word's intrinsic power? Could it be that in our earnest attempts to "be with" others in their suffering we have actually taken on their doubts and confusion? Have we forgotten that God's word is an alien and uncontrollable word, a word that even in coming to us does not relinquish to us its sovereignty?

Word and Technique

How is this communication of the word to be done? For pastors, the most crucial part of our preparation for speaking a word of God is for each of us to develop for ourselves an intimate, daily-nourished relationship with the word, and hence a ministry that is not burned out in frantic doing. As pastoral carers we can be personally receptive to the power of the uncontrollable word to change lives radically and therefore speak with authentic confidence out of our own experience with the word's address. We can approach our ministry of the word as persons acquainted with the word.

In a day when people are literally bombarded with words on every side, many of us have learned to ignore words as much as possible, and even to mistrust their speaker. This is why the visible word is often so important at the beginning of a pastoral care relationship; it can help provide receptive soil for our verbal message. As we approach a person in need of care, it is generally best to focus first on establishing a relationship of trust marked by empathy and suspension of judgment, functioning primarily out of the visible word in a ministry of compassionate presence. To speak the word of grace or of judgment prematurely will in most cases serve only to alienate the person and close off the possibility of any hearing of the word. But once a relationship has taken hold, the minister no longer can be morally neutral (as most psychotherapies claim to be).[34] In fact, there will be times when the verbal word must be spoken, either to convict of sin or to proclaim release through the Incarnate One. Verbal proclamation occurs not only in sermons or the study of scripture; it is a central component of all ministry, not least of all pastoral care ministry.

Certain methods of communicating the word of God verbally in pastoral care have proven historically to be promising—Hasidic storytelling, recovering forms of church discipline that have contemporary relevance, relating parables, labeling experienced events in a way that recognizes the word's past and present work in a person's life, sharing the impact of the word of one's own life ("witnessing" revisited), using biblical narratives as models for living. All of these and more are best used gently—after a trust relationship has been established. After all, the purpose in our using them is not to manipulate or pressure the other person but to share something of personal importance to ourselves with this other person for whom we care so deeply.

Verbal expression of the word in any care situation will, of course, be handled quite differently depending on the distinctive personality of the carer and on the particular minister's unique relationship with God. Such expression will emerge from a stance that involves expectant listening to and for the word. It may take the form of our gently nudging the person torn by guilt to look toward the source of reconciliation, perhaps as a question, "Did Christ die on the cross for everyone except you?" Or it may involve the bearing of a message of hope and peace to a bereaved family in a way that goes beyond simply "being with" them. It could mean confronting a parishioner involved in soft white-collar crime with the full reality of "stealing," no matter how socially acceptable the practice. And of course there will be times when the introduction of a spoken word of God may even be superfluous, as Ebeling suggests:

The Word receives the most explicit character of a promise when the future of the one addressed is involved, and the speaker himself does not promise this or that, but himself, pledges himself and his own future for the future of the other, gives him his word in the full sense of giving a share in himself. And here is the reason for the ultimate failure of the Word among men. For what happens when one man promises himself to the other? For the most part the Word becomes the bearer and mediator of egotism, inner emptiness, or lies. Yet even at his best man cannot promise true future, that is, salvation, to the other. Only the Word by which God comes to man, and promises himself, is able to do this. That this Word has happened, and can therefore be spoken again and again, that a man can therefore promise God to another as the One who promises himself—this is the certainty of Christian faith. . . .

Word is expressed anew only when it is heard anew, with tense attention to how the traditional Word manages to make itself understood in the real circumstances to which our lives are exposed.[35]

Our concern in this chapter has been to correlate the word of God and pastoral care. The word, communicated to us and through us as God establishes relationship with us, is God's creative way of acting—of opening our future to us. Ever since Augustine, this word has been characterized as encountering us both verbally and visibly. Proclamation of the word of God occurs both through what we do (the visible word) and in our concrete articulations (the verbal word). The word, however, is not something that can be manipulated; it is an uncontrollable word, a sovereign word. In pastoral care our response is, with the parishioner, mutually to listen for the word and then also to speak it both verbally and visibly. Finally, the courage to speak the word of God in a culture where God-talk is passé and even taboo is best drawn from the well of our own daily-nourished trust relationship with that same word, the embodiment of God's encounter with humanity. Pastoral care is not a peripheral form of ministry. Like all ministry, it is at its core proclamation of the word.

NOTES

1. See pp. 21-23, and Thomas Oden, "Recovering Lost Identity," *Journal of Pastoral Care*, 34, March 1980, pp. 4-23.

2. See, e.g., G. Johannes Botterweck and Helmer Ringgren, *Theological Dictionary of the Old Testament*, trans. John Willis and Geoffrey Bromiley, vol. III (Grand Rapids: William B. Eerdmans, 1978), pp. 85-125; Gerhard Kittel, *Theological Dictionary of the New Testament*, trans. Geoffrey Bromiley, vol. IV (William B. Eerdmans, 1967), pp. 69-137; George Buttrick, ed., *The Interpreter's Dictionary of the Bible*, vol. IV (Nashville: Abingdon Press, 1962), pp. 868-72.

3. J. N. Sanders, "The Word," in *The Interpreter's Dictionary of the Bible*, vol. IV (Nashville: Abingdon Press, 1962), pp. 870-71.

4. Although the various theologians to whom I turned, Thurneysen and Luther, Bultmann and Schillebeeckx, Ebeling and Asmussen, differ extensively in theological background and opinion, they manifest a remarkable convergence of understanding on this topic.

5. Edward Schillebeeckx, "Revelation in Word and Deed," in *The Word: Readings in Theology*, eds. Gavin, Carney et al. (New York: P. J. Kennedy & Sons, 1964), pp. 257-58.

6. C. K. Barrett, *The Gospel According to St. John* (London: S.P.C.K., 1958), p. 61.

7. Gerhard Ebeling, *God and Word*, trans. James W. Leitch (Philadelphia: Fortress Press, 1967), p. 40.

8. Rudolph Bultmann, *Jesus and the Word*, trans. Louise P. Smith and Erminie H. Lantero (New York: Charles Scribner's Sons, 1958), p. 218.

9. Gerhard Ebeling, *The Nature of Faith*, trans. Ronald G. Smith (Philadelphia: Fortress Press, 1961), pp. 87-88.

10. Robert W. Jenson, *Visible Words* (Philadelphia: Fortress Press, 1978), pp. 28-29.

11. Ibid., p. 3.

12. Ibid., p. 36.

13. LW 37, 135-36.

14. Schillebeeckx, "Revelation in Word and Deed," p. 262.

15. Quoted in Eduard Thurneysen, *A Theology of Pastoral Care*, trans. Jack A. Worthington and Thomas Wieser (Atlanta: John Knox Press, 1962), p. 15.

16. Paul Tillich, "The Relevance of the Ministry in Our Time and Its Theological Foundation," in *Making the Ministry Relevant*, ed. Hans Hofmann (New York: Charles Scribner's Sons, 1960), p. 22.

17. Thurneysen, *A Theology of Pastoral Care*, pp. 66 and 11.

18. LW 41, 150.

19. See especially John Baillie, John T. McNeill, and Henry P. Van Dusen, gen. eds., *Library of Christian Classics* (Philadelphia: Westminster Press, 1955), vol. 18, *Letters of Spiritual Counsel*, ed. and trans. Theodore G. Tappert.

20. Thurneysen, *A Theology of Pastoral Care*, p. 115.

21. See above, pp. 23-25.

22. Charles V. Gerkin, *Crisis Experience in Modern Life* (Nashville: Abingdon Press, 1979), pp. 15-16.

23. Dietrich Bonhoeffer, *Ethics*, ed. Eberhard Bethge, trans. Neville H. Smith (New York: Macmillan, 1955), p. 126.

24. LW 37, 92.

25. John B. Cobb, Jr., *Theology and Pastoral Care* (Philadelphia: Fortress Press, 1977), p. 52.

26. LW 27, 249.

27. Quoted in John R. Loeschen, *Wrestling with Luther* (St. Louis: Concordia Publishing House, 1976), p. 31.

28. Thurneysen, *A Theology of Pastoral Care*, p. 128.

29. Dietrich Bonhoeffer, *Life Together*, trans. John W. Doberstein (New York: Harper & Brothers, 1954), pp. 105, 107.

30. Ebeling, *God and Word*, pp. 3-4.

31. Ibid., p. 34.

32. Ibid., p. 35.

33. Ibid., p. 10.

34. See above, pp. 26-30.

35. Ebeling, *The Nature of Faith*, pp. 190-91.

4. Correlating Theology and Ministry

Parish pastors have been heard to complain: "The trouble with you seminary professors is that you don't know what's going on in the parish. Your ivory-tower theology has little to do with the problems I encounter in my daily work. I guarantee that if you spent six months as an assistant here in my parish you'd soon be teaching things differently."

Professors in the practical field often echo the complaint: "The problem with so many of my colleagues in the classical fields is that they never make their teaching practical enough to be of help to their students. What good does it do to compare Luther and Barth on law and gospel when what we need is a theology that directly addresses the specific issues of ministry—a theology of death, of evangelism, of administration. Theologians must speak to the concrete realities of the parish."

To which professors in the classical fields have been heard to respond: "What do I know about psychology, church growth, conflict management, or spiritual formation? I have trouble enough just keeping up-to-date in my own specialty, without reading also in psychotherapy and Christian education. If theology is to have impact on pastoral ministry, it is you practical types who will have to bridge the gap between the disciplines."

The need for correlation between theology and practice is now widely recognized, but who owns the problem? Whose is the responsibility?

To correlate is simply to bring two discrete entities into mutual relation with each other. Correlating theology with the practice of ministry involves allowing the insights of theological thought to impinge upon, interact with, and influence the actual day-to-day tasks of ministry and vice versa! In other words, theological belief and the theological template discussed in chapter 2 should make a difference in how we think about the care we offer and in how pastoral care, religious education, and church administration are carried out. But encounters with people in the parish must correspondingly interact with, and influence, theology.

The pastors and seminary professors alluded to above are all concerned about the impact of theology, biblical studies, ethics, and church history on day-to-day life in the parish. Their laments, while here a bit overstated to highlight the issue, are expressive of what appears to be an inherent difficulty; the responsibility for correlating theology and the practice of ministry is often relegated, along with the attendant blame, to somebody else, while few people personally take up the challenge and seriously grapple with the task. There is a need for all of us in ministry, whether in seminary or parish, both pastors and professors, to participate in the process.

Cognition and Correlation

Some indeed have begun to address the topic, but in most cases their work till now has focused on developing methods of correlation.[1] However, a more basic issue underlying any study of method has to do with the cognitive sets used to process data. Our purpose in this chapter is not to propose yet another method for correlation, but to focus on the two forms of mental organization that are essential if correlation, by whatever method, is to occur. These two cognitive sets must be understood before any system of correlation can be implemented. Our description of them here draws heavily on recent research into the functioning of the human brain.

The Two Hemispheres of the Brain

In general the right side of the brain controls the left side of the body, while the left side of the brain controls the right side of the body. Investigation of patients who through illness or injury have suffered damage to one hemisphere of the cerebral cortex has provided considerable information about the separate functions of each of the two lobes.[2] For example, damage to the left lobe causes individuals to have difficulty using language; in some cases language has been totally lost. Damage to the right lobe, although affecting language very little, precipitates great difficulties in spatial awareness, such as the recognition of faces once familiar. Although speech and logic appear unhindered, the ability to dress oneself also may be greatly affected.

The study of cerebral commissurotomy patients likewise has contributed significant data on the different functions of these two lobes. This radical technique was developed in order to treat severe epileptics. It involves a surgical severing of the two hemispheres so that they operate independently of each other. For many patients the operation has provided great help in the control of seizures; additionally, it has allowed researchers to study the specialized functioning of the cortex's two hemispheres.

Although most of the early research involving interhemispheric commissures was performed on cats (and later on monkeys and chimpanzees), it was the study of human subjects who had undergone cortex-severing surgery that greatly advanced the knowledge of how differently the two lobes of the cerebral cortex function. A variety of ingenuous experiments have been used to detect these divergencies.[3]

An example is the now classic test by Roger Sperry in which a word such as *keycase* is flashed on a screen for 100 milliseconds or less. In a split-brain patient's left visual field (that area to the left of the center point that the subject is viewing), only the letters "k,e,y" are seen; the letters "c,a,s,e" appear only in the right visual field. Since the flashing of the word to split-brain patients is at intervals too quick for the subjects to move their eyes, the letters "k,e,y" are presented only to the left eye (and thus to the right hemisphere) while the letters "c,a,s,e" are presented only to the right eye (and thus to the left hemisphere). When patients were asked at one point in the experiment what they saw, they reported only the word *case*. However, when Sperry asked them to place their left hands in an opaque bag filled with various objects and by touch alone retrieve the object they had just seen flashed on the screen, they removed a key.[4]

Michael Gazzaniga comments on the results of such tests:

The thrust of this work demonstrates there is a sharp breakdown in communication between the hemispheres of visual, somato-sensory, motor, and cognitive information. Information presented to the left hemisphere was normally named and described while information presented to the right were nameless, and the left hemisphere was unable to say what the right hemisphere was seeing or doing. . . . The studies went on to show that there were suggestions of marked differences in the way the hemispheres processed information. . . . More recent work suggests the intriguing possibility that problems that can be solved by either mode are handled by quite different cognitive strategies as a function of which hemisphere works on the task.[5]

Two Modes of Processing Cognitive Data

The results of such studies help sketch a clearer picture not only of how the brain functions but also of how human cognition works. The findings seem to indicate that each hemisphere thinks in fundamentally different ways, each having its own memory. Each hemisphere has different information-processing rules, which lead to two different modes of knowing. But before discussing these let us look more closely at the differences in functioning between the two methods of thinking.

For most individuals (98 percent of all right-handed and about two-thirds of all left-handed persons), the left hemisphere of the brain processes information sequentially. It functions logically (although it can be illogical!) and analytically. It compares, measures, analyzes, and judges. It names things; in fact, language, both verbal and written, is a function of this hemisphere. The left brain, working on a linear scale, creates time; it distinguishes between past and future.

Thomas Blakeslee, referring to a conversation between two people, provides a good illustration of the differences between the left brain and the right brain:

The left brain generally responds to the literal meaning of the words it hears and will not even notice the meaning of inflection. The right brain perceives different aspects of the same conversation: tone of voice, facial expression, and body language are noticed while the words are relatively less important. This is a two-way process. The words are coming from the other person's left brain, and the tone of voice, facial expression, and body language are coming from his right brain. Thus, the conversation is going on simultaneously on two levels. In fact, when two people interact, they actually form two separate relationships: the memories and impressions formed by the left and right consciousnesses may be completely different.[6]

The right hemisphere processes body image and the body's orientation in space; it includes recognition of people by their physical features. As Blakeslee points out, it translates paralinguistic and body language. Thus the right hemisphere processes information holistically rather than sequentially. It receives and considers a large mass of information in a parallel way, without separately considering each individual factor. It performs a synthetic-Gestalt organization of sensory data such as is performed in the perception and interpretation of a painting or photograph.

Because of its parallel processing of information, the right hemisphere has been described as the center of intuition, imagination, and creativity. It appears that many scientific discoveries originate with a right brain "insight."

Max Planck, an early investigator in quantum theory, believed that the scientist, to be creative, needs "a vivid intuitive imagination for new ideas not generated by deduction, but by artistically creative imagination."[7] Robert Nebes puts it:

The organization and processing of data by the right hemisphere is in terms of complex wholes, the minor hemisphere having a predisposition for receiving the total rather than the parts. . . . [It] probably provides the neural basis for our ability to take the fragmentary sensory information we receive and construct from it a coherent concept of the spatial organization of the outside world—a sort of cognitive spatial map by which we plan our actions.[8]

Each lobe of the cortex has the potential for many functions, and both participate in most activities. They work in partnership in order to assure the total functioning of the person. Each hemisphere, however, also has the ability to inhibit the other in order to solve a particular problem. In fact, since confusion would often result if both hemispheres gave simultaneous readings of an event or problem, one or the other, according to Robert Ornstein, usually takes over:

How do these two modes interact in daily life? My opinion, and that of David Galin, is that in most ordinary activities we simply alternate between the two modes, selecting the appropriate one and inhibiting the other. It is not at all clear how this process occurs. . . . Clearly each of us can work in both modes—we all can move in space, we all can do both at once. . . . The two modes of operation complement each other, but do not readily substitute for one another.[9]

Discoveries about the differences between the two hemispheres of the cortex have been used to support all sorts of outlandish conclusions. Many interpreters have superimposed on the left or right lobe all that they think is wrong with other people. To some, the left brain has become the hemisphere of an "uptight" society characterized by rigid military types and impersonal bureaucrats, with its preference for doing as over against being and for thinking as over against feeling. The right brain, on the other hand, has become associated with the counterculture, with hippies and flower children, followers of Eastern religions, artsy dilettantes, or with those warm, open folk who say wonderful things but hardly ever get anything done.

In truth, the so-called "clerk mentality," rigidly and mechanically following procedures without question, is no more an example of the left-brain cognitive set than is the drifting and unproductive "dreamer" an example of the right-brain approach. Both distortions are equally irresponsible, perhaps better if facetiously labeled "no brain." The real promise of our new learnings about right-brain and left-brain modes is not in excusing no-brain mentalities by giving them socially acceptable generic names, but in enabling individuals to make fuller use of their innate capacities in both hemispheres.

Hemispheric Dominance

It appears that by the time they have reached adulthood most individuals are predisposed in their cognitive functioning to be dominated by one or the other of their two hemispheric lobes (a majority by the left lobe). This predilection to dominance raises interesting questions for the pastors and professors mentioned earlier. Could it be that certain disciplines, such religious studies as the Germanic schools of biblical criticism and other classic academic fields, tend to attract individuals who are dominated by left-brain cognitive processes? Rigorous scholarship often requires examination of minute details, splitting the whole into many pieces in order to complete a thorough sequential analysis. Maybe the classical fields of theology, while they can and do use right-hemisphere cognitive functioning, rely *primarily* on the left-hemisphere style of thinking.

On the other hand, such practical fields as liturgics and pastoral care may seem to draw individuals who have leanings toward the right-hemisphere approach. Our forte in pastoral care, for example, is likely to be listening, empathizing, "being with," offering warmth and openness. The words of a deeply troubled person cannot be split, parsed, and analyzed like a third-century text; they must be heard as a whole. The carer's empathy and emotional closeness take the place of analysis; words of comfort replace critical objectivity. While it cannot be denied that the left hemisphere too functions in pastoral care, perhaps it does so to a lesser extent than in the classical fields of theology. The question is one of dominance.

Is there indeed a kind of hemispheric physiological predestination involved here? The age-old environment-versus-heredity argument has certainly surfaced again in recent studies on brain function. Although genetic structure cannot be ignored in understanding hemispheric dominance, most recent findings suggest that environment also is significant. Joseph Bogen states the position of most brain researchers: "It is likely that some anatomical asymmetry underlies the potential for hemisphere specialization; but it is also clear that the extent to which the capacities are developed is dependent upon environmental exposure."[10] Artisan and accountant, biblical scholar and pastoral care specialist—individuals in various occupational groups cannot be differentiated by the pattern of their hemispheric cognitive processes (that is, they do not use totally different modes of thinking). Rather, these groups are distinguished by the degree to which they use (and possibly by their ability to use) the cognitive functions of one or the other of their hemispheres. Thus, although most adults have in fact a hemispheric predisposition, it is one derived primarily through learning. The powerful influence of environment must be given its due.

Bilateral Cognition

Since our hemispheric predispositions are not only genetic but also to a great extent learned, it seems reasonable to assume that a change in environmental conditions can lead to the possibility of change in our style of cognitive functioning. To some extent we may have to live with a tendency toward either a right-hemisphere or a left-hemisphere style of information encoding; however, it also is possible to create conditions within our environments and schedules whereby the fullest possible use is made of all our cognitive capacities.

Marcel Kinsbourne hypothesizes that the development of cerebral hemispheric proclivity evolves by increases in proficiency and, in each hemisphere, learning to give attention to contralateral stimuli.[11] In several studies undertaken to verify this thesis, it was observed that giving the left lobe a verbal task reduced the left-eye-field superiority for recognizing faces; additionally, presenting a face recognition problem to the right lobe reduced the right-eye-field visual superiority for words.[12] Therefore, one way to counteract a tendency for left-hemispheric dominance is to "prime the pump" of the right hemisphere by looking at pictures or listening to music. Likewise, for the right-hemisphere-dominant person, reading a book or listening to a lecture will set the stage for left-hemisphere activity. In such a way one can momentarily lessen the dominance of one side of the brain and allow greater freedom for the other to apply itself, and its particular system for encoding data, to a given problem.

A key to effective correlation of theology and the practice of ministry is to set up the conditions that lead to facility in both right-brain and left-brain processes—in other words, to bilateral cognition. The goal is to permit each hemisphere to handle those particular data processing situations that are most suited to its particular style rather than allowing one or the other hemisphere to dominate most of the time. This is especially important since the lobe that is dominant inhibits the functioning of the other, and when one side is "running the show" the other (which is superior in its own type of information processing) is suppressed. Bilateral cognition leads to more comprehensive thought since it allows each hemisphere to think in the manner for which it was designed.

Creative Thinking

One way to understand bilateral cognition is to look at Graham Wallas' outline of the process of creative thinking.[13] Wallas describes four stages of creative thought: preparation, incubation, illumination, and verification. During preparation, relevant information is collected and the problem is narrowed until the issues that must be dealt with are brought into focus. In the incubation stage, out-of-consciousness forces work on the problem; although the individual periodically concentrates on it for short periods of time, there can be no movement toward resolution since this is strictly a time of germination during which nothing appears to be happening. Illumination then occurs spontaneously or as a consequence of a conscious undertaking; here the intuitive functioning of the brain takes over, and frequently the results occur instantaneously rather than following a series of logical steps. Finally, the verification stage requires logical validation of intuitive discoveries and the construction of an organized method for presenting the results.

Clearly it can be seen that left-lobe cognitive functioning is required in preparation and verification, while the right lobe will dominate during incubation and illumination. The cooperative functioning of the left brain and the right brain is aptly illustrated in any author's writing process. After completing library research for a book or article and reviewing various conflicting publications on the subject, the writer does best to let the project rest for a time, without pressuring for immediate results or even a detailed outline. Then, perhaps during sleep, the long drive to work, a choir anthem, or even a class lecture, the thesis may come in a flash. That burst of enlightenment must be listened to and trusted. Only after it occurs does the author take pen and paper in hand, or keyboard and word processor, and put the insight into written form.

Correlating Intentionally

What makes the results of split-brain research significant for correlating theology and the practice of ministry is not so much the functional difference between the two hemispheres as the two different cognitive ways in which data is processed. For a person's theology to have an impact on ministerial practice (and vice versa), both sides of the brain are required. The process of correlation involves a back-and-forth movement between the cognitive processing systems of each hemisphere.

In pastoral care, for example, the left-hemispheric task of preparation is required to help the minister understand basic theological dogma and develop a theological template; the systematic analysis and sequential thinking of this lobe form categories and draw a system of beliefs from scripture and the tradition of the church. The right-hemispheric tasks of incubation and illumination allow the richness of personal experience, as it comes across to the pastor in concrete care and counseling situations, to exist side by side with the prior theological constructs. Since the right lobe processes data in a parallel rather than sequential manner, a wide variety of seemingly dissonant information can be processed at the same time. The "genius" of the right hemisphere is its ability cognitively to absorb such diverse things as the deep pain expressed by a suffering human being and the more abstract insights of a biblical or theological theme in such a manner as to give meaning to both of them.

The left-hemisphere verification stage of cognition is required to help put these right-hemisphere insights into words. The parishioner is thereby helped to understand what is experienced. Such verbal processing is also important for the minister. Unless the right hemisphere's output is cycled back and reintegrated with the conceptual constructs, our theological belief systems, only sequentially developed, will become arid, devoid of the richness of parallel-processed experience. The danger in ministry is that we may venerate either the left-hemisphere or the right-hemisphere encoding strategies and not allow bilateral cognition to proceed for reflection on theology and experience requires both.

It is possible intentionally to structure stages in experience and reflection—to shape our environment—in ways that will require *both* lateral functions of the brain, thus allowing for a dialogical flow of insights between our theology and our practice of ministry. Individuals who find themselves more prone to left-hemisphere modes of information processing need to stop the incessant analyzing that often paralyzes and stifles creativity. They need to be receptive to insights that arrive while they are not overtly working on a specific problem and to trust and nurture these solutions.

Listening to music, gardening, meditating, walking—even such a "mindless" undertaking as turning the crank of a mimeograph machine—can inhibit left-brain activity and allow the right hemisphere to process information. The disciplines of spiritual direction can be of great benefit. Structuring one's schedule to include such right-hemisphere "pump priming" activities will enhance right-brain functioning. And when the insight comes, often in a flash, it must not be lost. The inspiration can come in a variety of forms—a visual image, a sudden recollection, a burst of ideas. In a pastoral care visit it may arrive as a mental picture, a parable, or a story from scripture bubbling to the surface of consciousness. Structuring one's schedule to make room for such insight includes a readiness to receive and grasp it.

On the other hand, those whose bias is toward right-brain functioning will be able to include the benefits of left-hemisphere cognition by balancing their approach with disciplined scholarship (preparation) and with logical, measurable verification of insights. Individuals involved in pastoral care frequently fail to give adequate attention to the preparation stage, even dismissing it out of hand as a purely head-level operation. As a result, theological constructs often have had little or no effect on the pastoral care offered. To assist in the preparation stage, left-brain "pump priming" can be fostered by reading daily in scripture and theology. Likewise, some practitioners may neglect the crucial verification stage. In this connection, left-hemisphere activity can be fostered by the simple method of putting one's insights into written form. The experiences of ministry are indeed raw material for theological formulation, but only if the pastoral carer takes the time—if necessary scheduled and rigorously observed—to articulate and test insights gained from the caring experience. Verification is further enhanced through sharing our reflected insights with others who might profit from them.

Recent research into the functioning of the cerebral cortex thus suggests that we think in two distinct ways. These cognitive sets—one processing data sequentially, the other in a parallel and holistic manner—are both needed for an effective correlation of theology and the practice of ministry. Intentionally creating an environment and structuring a schedule in such a way that both left-hemisphere and right-hemisphere styles of processing are nourished can only enhance the impact of theology upon ministry and allow our day-to-day experiences of ministry to inform and shape our theology. The results of such intentionally enhanced correlation will be seen in the enriched meanings that begin to gather around specific themes once, perhaps, considered as being discretely *either* theological *or* practical.

NOTES

1. For further information on the method of correlating theology and the practice of ministry see Larry Graham, "Dimensions of Theological Interpretation in the Practice of Ministry," *The Iliff Review*, pp. 3-11; Walter J. Lowe, "Method Between Two Disciplines: The Therapeutic Analogy," *The Journal of Pastoral Care*, September, 1981, pp. 147-56; John Patton, "Clinical Hermeneutics: Soft Focus in Pastoral Counseling and Theology," *The Journal of Pastoral Care*, September, 1981, pp. 157-68; Robert A. Preston, "Hermeneutic Processes and Pastoral Care," *Lexington Theological Quarterly*, October, 1977, pp. 128-36; Charles R. Stinnette, Jr., "The Pastoral Ministry in Theological Perspective," *Criterion*, Winter 1965, pp. 3-9; and Herbert W. Stroup, Jr., "Psychology, Theology, and the Parish or Where the Twain Do Meet," *Dialog*, Spring 1977, pp. 123-27.

2. For a more extended discussion of the two hemispheres of the cerebral cortex see J. E. Bogen, E. D. Fisher, and P. J. Vogel, "Cerebral Commissurotomy: A Second Case Report," *Journal of the American Medical Association*, 1965, pp. 1328-29; J. E. Bogen and M. S. Gazzaniga, "Cerebral Commissurotomy in Man: Minor Hemisphere Dominance for Certain Visuospatial Functions," *Journal of Neurosurgery*, 1965, pp. 394-99; J. E. Bogen and P. J. Vogel, "Cerebral Commissurotomy in Man: Preliminary Case Report," *Bulletin of Los Angeles Neurological Society*, 1962, pp. 169-72; Michael S. Gazzaniga, *The Bisected Brain* (New York: Appleton-Century-Crofts, 1970); Michael S. Gazzaniga, "Brain Mechanism and Behavior," in *Handbook of Psychobiology*, eds. Gazzaniga and Colin Blakemore (New York: Academic Press, 1975), pp. 565-90; Steven Harnad et al, eds., *Lateralization in the Nervous System* (New York: Academic Press, 1977); Robert D. Nebes, "Direct Examination of Cognitive Function in the Right and Left Hemispheres," in *Asymmetrical Function of the Brain*, ed. Marcel Kinsbourne (London: Cambridge University Press, 1978), pp. 99-137; M. C. Wittrock, "Education and the Cognitive Processes of the Brain," in *Education and the Brain*,

seventy-seventh yearbook, Part II, National Society for the Study of Education, eds. Jeanne S. Chall and Allan F. Mirsky (Chicago: University of Chicago Press, 1978), pp. 61-102; M. C. Wittrock et al, *The Human Brain* (Englewood Cliffs, N.J.: Prentice-Hall, 1977).

3. For a history of recent brain research, see especially Gazzaniga, "Brain Mechanism and Behavior," pp. 565-73.

4. Roger W. Sperry, "Hemisphere Deconnection and Unity in Conscious Awareness," *American Psychologist*, October, 1968, pp. 723-33.

5. Gazzaniga, "Brain Mechanism and Behavior," p. 567.

6. Thomas R. Blakeslee, *The Right Brain: A New Understanding of the Unconscious Mind and Its Creative Powers* (Garden City, N.Y.: Anchor Press; Doubleday, 1980), pp. 28-29.

7. Ibid., p. 49.

8. Robert D. Nebes, "Man's So-Called Minor Hemisphere," in *The Human Brain*, ed. M. C. Wittrock, pp. 102-4.

9. Robert E. Ornstein, *The Psychology of Consciousness* (San Francisco: W. H. Freeman, 1972), p. 62.

10. Joseph Bogen, "Some Educational Implications of Hemispheric Specialization," in Wittrock, *The Human Brain*, pp. 144-45.

11. Marcel Kinsbourne, "Cerebral Dominance, Learning, and Cognition," in *Progress in Learning Disabilities*, vol. 3, ed. Helmerr Myklebust (New York: Grune & Stratton, 1975), pp. 201-18; and Kinsbourne, "The Control of Attention by Interaction Between the Cerebral Hemispheres," in *Attention and Performance*, vol. 4, ed. Sylvan Kornblum (New York: Academic Press, 1973), pp. 239-56; also, Kinsbourne, "The Mechanism of Hemispheric Control of the Lateral Gradient of Attention," in *Attention and Performance*, vol. 5, ed. Patrick M. A. Rabbitt and Stanislav Dornic (New York: Academic Press, 1975), pp. 81-97.

12. Danny Klein, Morris Moscovitch, and Carlo Vigna, "Attention Mechanisms and Perceptual Asymmetries in Tachistoscopic Recognition of Words and Faces," in *Neuropsychologia*, 1976, pp. 55-66.

13. Graham Wallas, *The Art of Thought* (London: Butler & Tanner, 1926).

5. Spiritual Direction

Theology, in its simplest definition, is the study of the relationship between God and humans. Unfortunately, theological scholarship, by its very nature can contribute to a distancing of the theologian from the very God who is the subject of study. How this can happen is understandable. Included among the tools of modern scholarship are such enterprises as the painstaking examination of manuscript fragments, the historical probing of minute details, and the defining and interrelating of a myriad of concepts. Most theological education divides the task of ministry into such discrete segments as biblical studies, dogmatics, languages, history, theological ethics, social ethics, public speaking, psychology, sociology, pastoral care, religious education, and church administration.

In seminary, students experience a broad range of courses, each having a particular slant, each affording a different sense of the gospel and of ministry. Each course is offered by an expert who has delved more deeply into that particular subject area than you or I ever will.

Much of the scholarship has been performed for us. Thus the study of theology carries with it an implicit problem: The methodologies inherent in most of its disciplines—form-critical, historical, archaeological—lend themselves to a distancing from the content. This distancing must occur. A critical stance is necessary if one is to gain a more accurate understanding of the object being studied, but there can be an attendant loss. The intimacy of the God-person relationship can be displaced by the methodological tendency to segment, parse, and observe from an objective distance. Wolfhart Pannenberg comments on this loss in academic theology:

But authentic theology has always been distinguished . . . by its ability to speak to central motifs of the Christian faith. These are not simply matters of doctrine, such as the Trinity, the cross and resurrection of Jesus Christ, God's kingdom, and faith itself. Such doctrinal issues are indeed related to the dynamic life of Christian faith, but when treated in separation from their experiential roots they can represent little but the deadwood of an old tradition.[1]

His comment is not intended as a criticism of theology or of theological scholarship. There is no implication that "if only the seminaries would teach this or that," then such problems would be resolved. The scholarly methodologies are needed. They give us a clearer grasp of scripture and its message and of the worlds to which that message is addressed.

Indeed, the problem is not so much the methods employed in contemporary theology as the lack of correspondingly effective methodologies by which Christians can foster the development of their relationship with God. Where the "experiential roots" to complement rigorous theological methods are lacking, a serious gap results. Don Browning has pointed out that in previous eras of the church methods of Christian living were relied upon to feed spiritual growth and moral development, and that the absence of such methodologies within the church today presents a real crisis.[2]

I would not advocate a return to the era of pietism, when often an individual's relationship with God was considered the only important aspect of faith. Reinvolvement in social ministry and social action was desperately needed if the church was to regain its prophetic role in the world. However, as critical as it surely is for Christians to take a stand on issues that affect society and the natural world, if we lose touch with our "base"—our faith in and our intimate relationship with that world's Creator and Redeemer—then our pronouncements will be empty and our solutions temporary, and we will be dangerously subject to the vagaries of social and political fashion, speaking a word rather than the word to our troubled time.

Given the modern de-emphasis on the Christian's relationship with God, however, and the dearth of methods for fostering spirituality, the church and its clergy are in danger today of moving toward a pre–Reformation orientation in which the pastor authoritatively tells the faithful what to believe and do, while the faithful themselves abdicate their responsibility of striving to hear the word (the minister does that for them!).

Such a shortcut has its advantages, for confusion and disagreement easily occur where a whole congregation is trying as individuals to discern the word and will of God. Certainly it is clearer if the task of discernment is undertaken only by the minister, the faith specialist. But the shortcut of specialization is also dangerous. All Christians need to grow in the Spirit; all need to listen carefully for the word. And, given this age's lack of methodologies for Christian living, all Christians need assistance in accomplishing that task.

Krister Stendahl has reminded us that God is always present to us, that we operate each day in the face of God.[3] Throughout its history the church has depended on "spiritual direction" to help heighten people's awareness of that presence. Spiritual direction, in brief, is concerned with awareness of and growth in one's relationship with God. It has reference to a place—a person, actually—where Christians can go to talk specifically about that relationship. It suggests a method of pastoral care that sensitizes people to that presence of God that already exists, in which we live.

Direction and Correlation

If the correlation of theology and pastoral care is our purpose, then spiritual direction must be our concern. It is an important bridge between theology and care. It focuses on our relationship with God, that factor in human experience from which we draw meaning, the courage to be, and the power to live an authentic life. For the ministers, spiritual direction may provide a way whereby we can return to the sources of our faith, reflecting on theology and on our experience of God. It prepares us for the automatic responses that are required in the care we give, to which we referred in the final section of chapter 1. Spirituality is not a matter of detached reflection, as some may think; it involves a relationship, a gift of grace. That relationship is determined by the Giver to be sure, yet is dependent on the recipient's active response to the gift.

Spiritual direction reminds us that a relationship with God is the overarching concern that focuses all others (while not negating or replacing them), that it helps us rise beyond our basic human needs and wants to follow the Spirit's leading. In fact, spiritual direction is one method by which what is discussed in theology classes or read in theological discourses can have a direct impact on the ministry we offer. It is a place where doctrines such as sin, finitude, forgiveness, and grace can be discussed *and experienced*. Frequently the pastor helps parishioners recognize that what they are going through—for example, release from guilt over a certain offense—is what the liturgy, sermon, and scripture are really talking about, in this case, forgiveness. Thus, spiritual direction serves an interpretive function in pastoral care.

The point was made in chapter 1 that pastoral care and counseling have benefited tremendously from learnings in psychiatry, psychotherapy, and psychology over the last sixty years. These learnings have revolutionized the care we offer. Psychology has taught us much about underlying motives, human development, how people change, and how relationships are established. Through such learnings our care has become more sensitive. The current resurgence of attention to spiritual direction can have a similar impact on pastoral counseling and care. It can provide tools to assist us and our parishioners in our quieting and centering, so that we all become more receptive to others, the universe, and the word. It can teach us effective ways of utilizing such spiritual resources as scripture, prayer, journals, and meditation.

People who are obsessed with themselves and their own problems can benefit from becoming absorbed instead in faith's larger concerns.

Whether or not pastors actually do spiritual direction as such, its influences, like the influences of psychology, can infuse our entire ministry to people. Certainly it can help us regain a lost or forgotten part of our ministerial heritage, defuse the cricitism that pastoral counseling is nothing but "warmed-over psychology" and enable us to guide people's growth in the most important relationship of life, their relationship with God.

Such growth has been a concern of the church from the very beginning. Paul distinguishes between the *nepioi*, those beginners in the faith ("babes in Christ") who are fed only milk, and the *teleioi*, those more "mature" Christians who can receive solid food (I Cor. 3:1-2, cf. 2:6, 13-16; Eph. 4:13-15; cf. Col. 1:10). In my view the church today, especially among Protestants, may be focusing too intently on the *nepioi*. We hear too many introductory lectures, too much, "This is what we should be doing in [our lives, the ghetto, Central America]." There is not enough nourishing of the faithful to a deeper understanding of the gospel and a more significant relationship with God.

Spiritual direction, however, and the learnings that flow from it, can help people grow and mature in their faith. Such growth is essential; the *teleioi* are those who have moved from the way of the flesh to the way of the spirit, whereby self-centeredness is transformed into compassion and a sense of unmerited gift. The *teleioi* are hopeful for the full revelation of God, a hope that encourages patience in suffering. If our pastoral care is aimed solely toward meeting people's needs, then our ministry will be dominated by the most obvious needs that come before us—people in situational crises who may want only a quick bandage put over their wounds so they can go on their way. But, as C. W. Brister has noted, pastoral care ministry comes out of both the push and the pull of the faith. It requires us to respond to people's needs, of course, but also to help people face the needs and commands of the gospel.[4] Surely pastoral care ministry is offered to the *nepioi*, but it must foster spiritual growth for the *teleioi* as well.

History and Terminology

In the Roman tradition, and to a considerable degree in the Anglican, the practice of giving care for the life of the spirit has generally come under the rubric of spiritual direction (its theoretical companion variously classed as ascetic, mystical, or spiritual theology). In most of Protestantism there has been no regularly accepted term for the same reality. "Devotional life" and "faith development" perhaps come closest. Historically, the church has referred to the person of the spiritual director as: spiritual friend, spiritual companion, spiritual guide, soul friend, ghostly counselor, and spiritual mother or father. "Spiritual direction" and "director" (or simply pastor) will be used here because they are most commonly accepted. In the field as a whole there are a variety of perspectives, or schools, of spiritual direction, such as Franciscan, Eastern, and Carmelite.[5] I am impressed, above all, with the Ignatian perspective, though I have also learned much from contemporary directors trained in pastoral counseling and psychotherapy.

Spiritual direction especially in the form of contemplative or meditative prayer, has a centuries-old history. Its roots go as far back as the devotional life of ancient Jewish communities such as the Therapeutae and the Essenes. Spiritual disciplines also are found in the contemplative practices of many Eastern religions. Indeed, early Christian techniques for relaxing, stilling, and breathing have their parallels in the practices and rites of a number of "primitive" peoples, such as the northern-plains Indians in the United States, nomadic Eskimos in Canada and Russia, and several tribes in Africa.

The spiritual disciplines of the church can be traced back as far as the fourth-century desert fathers and mothers. In Egypt, Syria, and Palestine the early Christians sought out hermit monks as guides for the godly life. Since then, each century has had its cherished guides: Jerome, Catherine of Siena, John of the Cross, Ignatius of Loyola, Teresa of Avila, Martin Luther, Francis de Sales.

Pastoral care has long focused on the parishioner's relationships—with self, family and other persons, the universe, and God. Spiritual direction concentrates particularly, though not exclusively, on the relationship with God. Except for Roman Catholics and Episcopalians, few have written on the topic in recent years. The purpose of this chapter is to provide a brief sketch of spiritual direction, especially for those pastors whose previous experience with it may have been quite limited.[6]

As has already become apparent, for pastoral care two terms bear special importance in any understanding of spiritual direction: "religious experience" and "relationship with God." Religious experience is not altogether familiar to many of us late-twentieth-century travelers. For one thing, most of us have probably given more attention to ethics or action than to the interiority of the religious life. Then too, movements into psychological interiors or toward more abstract theological articulation have tended to ignore spirituality. A different language is needed, a terminology that is relational because it talks about relationships, religious because the relationships in question involve God, and concrete because the focus is on the specific reality of that particular relationship.

By "relationship with God" I mean that we are creatures, whether we know it or not, and God is our creator. If we are unaware of our createdness we may experience it as rootlessness, loneliness, a sense of being lost. The lack may also show itself positively, in a yearning for some deeper sense of meaning in life that cannot be named. Spirituality always has at its base a relationship in which God reaches out to us, offering himself as a gift. William Barry puts it this way:

It should be obvious that this kind of spiritual direction makes a radical assumption in faith; namely, that the Lord is actually and actively engaged now with his people as individuals, that he desires their intimacy, and that his people can experience that intimacy.

Moreover, it assumes that such a desire for intimacy is for the benefit of his people.[7]

Thus spirituality begins with God, God as gift. Spiritual direction is the art of helping others discern that gift and respond to it. Such direction usually occurs in a one-to-one, contractual relationship between director and directee, though there are historical and contemporary precedents for group direction. Most group guidance has been for families or celibate associations. Prayer groups also have sometimes served not only to bring human concerns to God but also to train people in the life of the Spirit. Some directors even believe that group guidance may be the most important form of spiritual care, from the standpoint of using our time efficiently and of building community.

William Connolly furthered our understanding of spiritual direction when he wrote:

"Spiritual" does tell us that the basic concern of this kind of help is not with external actions as such, but with the inner life, the "heart," the personal core out of which come the good and evil that men think and do. It includes "head," but points to more than reason and more than knowledge. It also reminds us that another spirit, the Spirit of the Lord, is involved. "Direction" does suggest something more than advice-giving and problem-solving. It implies that a person who seeks direction is going somewhere, and wants to talk to someone on the way. It implies, too, that the talk will not be casual and aimless, but have to help him find his way.[8]

In spiritual direction one has a companion who supports and confronts, a guide who helps form one's life with God, and so also with other people and even with the universe. Its focus is on the inner life. Its result is to transform our living and lead to action, responsible service, and moral living.

Such direction helps people search for and find meaning, the lack of which is a major cause of the modern malaise. Carl Jung noted that much neurotic behavior in people over the age of thirty-five results from ignoring experiences of meaning. Indeed, Jung states, one of the reasons he studied this area of experience so extensively was that he could not find clergy who were equipped or willing to deal with it.[9]

Spiritual direction enables individuals to get beneath their own surface conventions and attitudes about life. Its focus is heavily upon experience; though not anti-intellectual, it is primarily a school of the heart. Direction is a place where the God-person relationship can be talked about seriously, a rare thing in our post–Christian culture, where such talk is often experienced as an embarrassment. Indeed, to quote William A. Barry and William J. Connolly: "Spiritual direction may be considered the core form from which all forms of pastoral care radiate, since ultimately all forms of pastoral care and counseling aim, or should aim, at helping people to center their lives in the mystery we call God."[10]

Relation to Psychotherapy and Pastoral Counseling

Spiritual direction is similar in many ways to pastoral counseling and psychotherapy but also dissimilar. Gerald May has suggested a helpful way to highlight the comparison and contrast. He offers three short monologues—one from humanistic psychotherapy, one from pastoral counseling, and one from spiritual direction.[11]

In psychotherapy one might say, "I bring all that I am into this relationship with you. For the time we are together I attend to you with all my heart, and with all my expertise. I give my attention to our being together in the hope that this will facilitate your growth and health."

In pastoral counseling the parallel statement might be, "In the name of God I am here for you. I give my attention to you and to our being together as a representative of God's love and care for you. I am a broken, human expression of that love, but you have my attention and care while we are together, and my prayers while we are apart."

And in spiritual direction the statement might be, "My prayers are for God's will to be done in you and for your constant deepening in God. During this time that we are together I give myself, my awareness and attention and hopes and heart *to God for you. I surrender myself to God for your sake."*

These monologues may be oversimplified. After all, every director practices the art in a unique way, usually from the perspective of one of the various "schools" of spiritual direction, and refined explorations of the similarities and differences are available, but May's simple monologues make vivid some crucial ways in which spiritual direction is unlike either pastoral counseling or psychotherapy.[12]

The most significant distinction of spiritual direction is its focus on developing and strengthening one's personal relationship with God. Relationships with therapist, spouse, family, friends, colleagues, and others in one's life, though not ignored, are all secondary.

Shaun McCarty notes a second difference: "The focus in counseling is more on problem solving, on effecting better personal integration and adjustment in the process of human maturation. The focus in spiritual direction, on the other hand, is more on growth in prayer and charity."[13] In other words, the criteria by which success is judged are also different. In counseling or therapy, success is based primarily on achieving the client's wishes, meeting agreed-upon goals, or attaining a certain level of mental health (unless of course the client wants to achieve something utterly unrealistic or perhaps even illegal). But in spiritual direction the criteria for judgment are faithfulness to the call of God, Christian virtues such as Paul frequently listed in his letters, service to the entire Christian community, and above all a heightened sensitivity to the inner murmurings of God's Spirit.

Other differences between spiritual direction and therapy/pastoral counseling might also be mentioned, such as the director's training, charismatic office, and distinctive techniques. That direction also bears resemblances to the other two forms of help, of course, can never be denied. Especially in recent years when directors have begun receiving psychological training, the lines between them have even become somewhat blurred. Robert Rossi makes the point: "Granted the important distinctions, what makes for good counseling makes for good direction: expertise with warmth. When the director's theological and spiritual insight is coupled with his psychological sensitivity, he stands ready to effectively exercise the *cura animarum.*"[14]

For pastoral care, the ideal would seem to be a pastor trained in pastoral counseling who has learned from psychotherapy and has developed skill in spiritual direction. Pastors so equipped, while they may only rarely offer classical spiritual direction, will in their care and counseling be better able to ascertain just what the seeking person needs and just where to begin. My vision is that ministers, particularly Protestant pastors who are not very familiar with spiritual direction, will discover it, learn from it, grow in their own disciplines of prayer, and allow these disciplines to affect the care they offer. Spiritual direction can constitute an excellent environment for the correlating of pastoral care and theology, for unhurried reflection on the experience, and source, of our own faith. By reincorporating spiritual direction into its practice, pastoral care and counseling can significantly realign itself with its religious heritage.

Beginning the Process

Jung's observation that many people in the second half of life struggle with issues of meaning certainly applied to Charles Monti, the forty-nine-year-old owner of a hardware store in a small midwestern town. Monti's wife had died four years before, about the time his second and last son left for college in the East. Her death had left Monti with many questions. Outwardly life continued as usual. His business was running smoothly, managed now by his first son. At long last he had the leisure to do things he had always wanted to do but could not do because of family and business. He made regular trips to Minnesota and Canada for fishing and to Wisconsin for deer hunting. He had always been a believer, an active church attender and supporter, and had even taught church school classes on and off for years. He liked working with young people and, while his two sons were teenagers, assisted as a sponsor of the youth group. Monti was the type of church member every pastor likes to have in the congregation and says, "You can always count on Chuck. Whether you need a helping hand or something from his store, he always says yes."

So it was with some surprise that Pastor Karen Jonsered, on asking the widower if he would help organize a church clean-up day, heard him say instead, "I'd like to talk with you sometime, I mean if you've got the time."

"Sure, I've always got time for you, Chuck. What is it?"

"Oh, it's hard to explain. I'm a little confused and I'm not just sure what I want to do."

Pastor Jonsered could not imagine what was on Chuck's mind; he did not seem upset or confused. In fact, during the last few years he had appeared more relaxed and at peace than she ever remembered. They made an appointment.

Once in the pastor's office, Monti poured out his story. True, he was more relaxed than ever. He was doing things he had always dreamed of doing—and even now was planning a fishing trip to Alaska for the following summer. He liked having more recreational opportunities, missed his wife, dated now and then ("but how many women are you going to find in a small town like this?") but had no plans for marriage. "Ever since we finished the Bethel Bible Series," he said, "I've wondered if something is missing in my life. I really liked the study of the Bible and sometimes wish I could become a better Christian. Sometimes I feel empty inside and wish that I felt more like I was doing what God intends for me."

Already pastoral assessment was taking place. Pastor Jonsered pondered some possibilities: Is Chuck suffering from a stalemated grief? Depression? Guilt for some secret past or present sin? Is he just bored with all of his new free time? Is his a case of mid-life crisis? Is he too dependent? Is the problem a matter of vocational crisis? Does he want to go into the ordained ministry? Maybe none of the above? Actually, the pastor found traces of *all* of the above in Monti's expressions of uneasiness, but none seemed of significant weight. She met with him several times trying to sort things out.

Pastor Jonsered had become interested in spiritual direction while attending seminary and had received two years of direction from an Episcopal priest. She soon began to wonder if direction might not be helpful to Monti, for already by their third visit together he was repeatedly raising questions about prayer, his feelings toward God, and his concerns about not being active enough in the church. Pastor Jonsered suggested that they spend some time helping him develop his life of prayer. "I think you're searching. You seem to be looking for something more in your relationship with God and the church than what you have right now." Monti agreed. "I'd like you to consider something called spiritual direction," she went on. "It helps people grow in their prayer life and their relationship with God."

When people come specifically in quest of guidance for their spiritual life or "to be closer to the Lord," it is crucial, as in all pastoral counseling, that the pastor determine what really has prompted their appearance. This does not mean that their first expressions of desire for spiritual help should not be taken seriously—to the contrary—but it is always important for ministers to ascertain whether those first-stated desires for help are accurate, or are only a way of asking for something else (perhaps money, prayers, help in dealing with guilt, legal or medical care, or just a listening ear). In addition to asking what must obviously be asked first in theological assessment, "Why are they coming to *me?*" it is necessary to ask, "Why are they coming *now?*" (See chapter 2.) And it is good to get some sense of what they expect to receive from the spiritual help they are requesting.

Clearly, pastors who offer direction must determine whether the individual is capable of undertaking spiritual direction. This is not to say that only the fit, educated, and emotionally healthy can be involved in spirituality. The history of the church would argue against that; some of the most notable saints, after all, were known to skirt the borders of craziness! However, not all people are able or willing to take the step of entering direction. They may lack sufficient belief in God and prayer or the ability to experience their inner world; they may be incapable of reflection on experience or unable to relax sufficiently to listen for the still small voice; or they may have pressing problems in life that make it difficult to focus on anything else.

A first session in spiritual direction can begin very much like a first session in pastoral counseling, a process that I have described elsewhere.[15] The pastor seeks first to establish a solid relationship with the parishioner, one that allows give-and-take between the two. By the time Charles Monti decided to enter into spiritual direction, he and Pastor Jonsered could already build not only on their years of friendly association but also on the several counseling sessions in which they had explored the reasons for his bewildering uneasiness. Instead of continuing to discuss his "problem," Monti now talked with the pastor about his decision to proceed. He shared with her some background of his life and faith. Such sharing is important. Pastors cannot assume that their prior association with a parishioner active in the church automatically gives them insight into that individual's faith and inner struggles.

In general, people who have come for direction are not beginners in the faith; most have attained some degree of maturity. The pastor begins by trying to help them focus on and clarify their past religious experiences. Most people are rather inarticulate when they first try to express their deeper feelings and beliefs. The request to "tell me about your relationship with God in prayer" can totally "stump" some people, even those who are able to speak concretely and subjectively about their relationships with other people. Frequently directees will rely on purely objective descriptions, or theological formulas learned long ago. This inarticulateness poses a barrier that may crumble only slowly; the process can rarely be accelerated. Early on, therefore, parishioners need help in learning to look at, notice, and then actually express what they "see" in the world of their own experience. This began for Charles Monti, as it usually does in spiritual direction, with those initial explorations of what caused him to ask for help. Only after extensive discussion of his seemingly barren prayer life could director and directee get at the concrete facts about who God is to him, and how he responds to God.

The Contemplative Attitude

One of the most important initial tasks of the director is to help new directees form a "contemplative attitude," i.e., pay attention to their own inner experience. The contemplative attitude includes a looking for and listening to another voice. It means an attentiveness to the word, to the presence that already exists but needs to be recognized. This approach to prayer represents a major shift in attitude for many people. It means a movement away from self-absorption toward immersion in the Other. It involves listening a good deal less to one's own self-talk or obsessions and more to the presence of God. Without such a contemplative attitude, growth in the spiritual life will be stunted. Most efforts to enhance our spiritual life through various disciplines are, like the growing branches on a giant pine, dependent on this base of receptiveness and openness to the movements of the Spirit within us—the sunshine and rain of God's presence in our lives.

Some methods of helping people develop the contemplative attitude can backfire. The person intentionally trying to pray and "get closer to God" can easily end up frustrated and even more self-obsessed. A way to circumvent this frustration is to urge directees to do things they enjoy, things that are naturally engaging. Such activities may include walks on the beach or in the woods, listening to Bach, looking at a sunrise or sunset, watching a thunderstorm run its course, playing a musical instrument, even long-distance running. The activity must be one that is greatly absorbing. For me, walking quietly in the woods or fishing (staring for hours at a bobber that doesn't move) have been just such activities. They seem to foster contemplation.

Situations in which I find myself have also been catalytic at times. About a dozen years ago I started arriving a day early to any conference I planned to attend. The American Association of Pastoral Counselors usually met in big cities that were largely unfamiliar to me, so I would hit the streets immediately after arrival and, except for sleep, I'd walk for the next twenty-four hours without saying a word to anyone. In the midst of all that hustle and bustle, people rushing this way and that, I would walk aimlessly—observing, listening, thinking, feeling, without a word. I miss those walks, now that they are no longer possible. Such contemplative moments can be redemptive. Each of us will find our own ways to open up and forget about ourselves.

Such experiences seemed already built-in so far as Charles Monti's life was concerned. The pastor encouraged him to "let the Lord share these experiences with you." She expressed confidence that God would make God's presence known in time, that Monti only needed to listen for it and be aware of it when it happened. "God is a friend who will be with you in every experience of life, even when the hamburger juices are dripping down your wrist at the lunch counter. God is the kind of presence you might feel with a close personal friend, only it's *always* there." Monti was urged to take a let-it-happen attitude, not trying to force anything. Unlike Charles Monti, some people may be knotted up with tension and anxiety; relaxation or breathing exercises such as I have described elsewhere,[16] may help them become more receptive.

Directees are asked to reflect, after periods of involvement in each such naturally engaging activity, on just what has happened. They need not expect fantastic or deeply religious experiences, but only review honestly and openly what actually occurred—thereby learning to be aware of and to reflect on the quiet movements of the Spirit. People learn that God speaks not only when they are on their knees but also in life's daily events. Experience comes first, then reflection. They are led to ask: "How has the Lord made his presence known to me? In what ways did the Spirit speak?" Parishioners need to know that this shift in our orientation to prayer takes time, because most of us tend to pray in ways that do not actively foster awareness of God; usually our lives are so busy that we do not pause at all to reflect on God's activity in our midst. The contemplative attitude needs nurturing. New skills and disciplines are not developed overnight.

Writing Activities

In some instances it is a helpful practice at the outset for directees to write a history of their spiritual journey. They should have no worry that they have not been "holy" enough. Rather they are simply to write about their life of faith, including their practice of prayer. Such writing enables the pastor to become better acquainted with their spiritual life, and directees in turn are stimulated to begin the process of remembering and reflecting on their inner experience.

While such writing activities may be positive for some parishioners, the director will want from others a more extensive background before proceeding with the direction process. In such cases a variation of Ira Progoff's written dialogue process could prove helpful.[17] The pastor may ask the directees to close their eyes and try to image their own spiritual journey as that of a person other than themselves, then open their eyes and write a script of the journey. This is to be done as rapidly as possible, until the writing comes to a natural break or pause. They can then share with the pastor any or all of the written material, as they wish, and it can be used to explore meanings in the directees' lives.

In the case of Charles Monti, he had done little or no writing in his entire lifetime, short of a note scrawled on an invoice or a brief message to one of his employees. His wife had always taken care of the family's correspondence, and his outside interests were far from the literary realm. Surprisingly, perhaps because of its very unfamiliarity, writing became for Monti a way to express ideas and emotions he had never verbalized. Throughout he was helped to discover much about his own spirituality that he had not previously recognized or understood.

Structuring the Sessions

Once the getting-to-know-you period is over and spiritual direction is well underway, a typical session usually begins with silence—perhaps five to ten minutes of silence—during which one or more, possibly new, spiritual disciplines are used (we will mention some of them in the sections that follow). One or both of the participants might audibly pray.

Pastor and parishioner talk about their reactions to whatever discipline was used in the period of silence and then move on to a discussion of developments in the person's relationship with God as experienced since the previous session. Special attention is often given to one's prayer experiences. The pastor may then reflect aloud on what has been expressed, as in a pastoral counseling session.

Frequently such discussion and reflection are all that is required. At other times the director may make suggestions to assist with the person's growth in prayer. Recommended may be the use of additional disciplines or specific portions of scripture that could be of help in attempts at contemplative prayer. At times, pastors may wish to interpret what is happening or try to help the individual through a particular spiritual crisis, such as emotional dryness in prayer.

Spiritual direction sessions generally occur less frequently than counseling sessions. Indeed, after a few initial weekly meetings at which pastor and directee are getting acquainted, direction is likely to take place only once every three or four weeks.

Spiritual Disciplines

A variety of disciplines—methods, techniques—have already been mentioned as being useful in connection with spiritual direction. They facilitate openness in one's relationship with God. Prayer, journals, scripture, and meditation serve such purposes. Each can be a fruitful resource for developing the contemplative attitude. There is not room here to cover these disciplines in the detail they deserve but only to introduce them.

Prayer

Prayer is the most important of the disciplines. In fact, some practitioners think of spiritual direction as essentially a school of prayer. William Barry points out that many people have great difficulty praying; they think of prayer in a stylized manner, and as a result find it a barren experience. Some ways of praying are helpful, he suggests, while others are not. Prayer motivated by obligation or duty rarely leads to wholeness and life and is often smothered in the tedium or boredom that ensues. Similarly, prayer that is primarily a matter of petitions, thinking, or making resolutions does not lead to the enthusiasm of a love relationship.[18] Indeed, for many people, prayer is so concentrated on self—on one's own sins, problems, strivings, wants or wishes—that they are prevented from really listening and seeing. If a man overwrought with grief and guilt for "bringing my marriage down by having an affair" is obsessed by his own wrongdoing, he will have difficulty seeing the great deeds that God has done, the forgiveness that God offers, and the new life that comes as a gift.

It can take a considerable time and much practice to make the shift from self-centered prayer to openness and listening. Prayer should cease being a matter of duty and become instead a joy, a looked-for event. It is not a chore, like doing the dishes or being audited by the IRS. The woman who still prays like an eight-year-old will not easily tell God her rage at the loss of her husband. She needs guidance in her relationship with God, not glib suggestions to "get your anger out." Years of habit and training cannot be undone in a week or a month. It may be helpful to refer such people to the psalmists' expressions of anger and impatience at God, or to biblical examples of "improper" requests (such as the story of the blind Bartimaeus in Mark 10), or to helpful books on prayer. Such people need painstaking and compassionate help as they gradually become aware of unwanted feelings toward God and toward creation, and are increasingly able to speak to God about the truth they discover.

Relationships can develop only when the parties involved pay attention to each other. Christian tradition assures us that God does his part, attending always to each of us. The believer, therefore, where relationship to God is to be developed, must attend to God. We human beings have enough trouble even noticing, let alone caring for, anyone else, without the added difficulty of paying attention to the invisible, mysterious God. Contemplative prayer means becoming increasingly absorbed in God and the person of Jesus.

Pastoral carers have a keen eye for the quality of an individual's relationships. The pastor doing direction likewise keeps an eye on the character of the relationship between the directee and God, as evidenced in prayer. Many of the same dynamics that affect communication in marriage also affect communication between people and God. The pastor skilled in relationship counseling will, for example, be able to discern when an individual is keeping certain feelings or issues hidden, keeping God at a distance by using words that are highly impersonal. In fact, a person's words (especially the words of address) often disclose a great deal about how that person views God—as an angry and distant parent, a good but impotent friend, a time-management expert who watches our every move, even a "typical male."

Prayer time is not always a peaceful time. In my experience prayer can be quite troubling, unnerving, discomforting. Parishioners who are mature in their faith and have moved beyond God as a bad parent commonly tell of a relationship that appears dry, flat, even distant, of the kind one sees when relatives gather unwillingly for some obligatory family occasion. They are uncomfortable, uninterested in the other people, and cannot wait until they get seated for dinner. Some of them sit around in overstuffed chairs with dazed and faraway looks on their faces while others attempt a little pained and awkward small talk.

When this dreadful kind of relationship infects the life of prayer, the pastor must gently question directees to determine causes of the distance and dryness. "What are your feelings now?" "What are the things you are not saying to God?" Questions can often open up the channels of communication and insight. When it appears that emotions will not flow easily, I have sometimes used a Gestalt chair dialogue, with God occupying the empty chair.[19] Once people begin to unload to the pastor and express feelings, it is helpful to suggest that they say these things to God. What they thought they were saying only to the pastor, they now find they are communicating to God—that is prayer! Prayer must mean something significant to us, or it amounts to no more than party chitchat or the selfish requests of a child.

Methods that help ease our experience of dryness in relationship with God are not to be regarded as magic potions. Winter seasons are to be expected in the life of prayer, whether we are in spiritual direction or not, and they will not always change to summer as quickly as we might wish.

In human relationships intimacy is fostered by regular engagement. So too with prayer. A person wishing to share an intimate relationship with the Redeemer may need to develop a discipline of prayer, such as setting aside a regular time where the mind's clutter subsides and a listening for the word occurs. Such a set time period may be especially helpful during the early months of direction. Those who never have mastered daily prayer might be invited initially to undertake a consistent pattern, one that can be continued on a permanent basis later. They should be cautioned, however, that the most common mistake is to start big. In terms of both frequency and length of prayer periods a small undertaking is best, one that can be sustained on a regular, perhaps daily basis. More important than how often and how long is the attitude with which we approach this separate time, as an opportunity simply to "be," specifically to be with a close Friend and appreciate the gift of life, allowing our striving egos to relax and our overtaxed feelings to experience calm.

Words are not absolutely essential in prayer. Some beginners on the journey of prayer may not be able to move from voiced petitions to wordless prayer immediately—nor need they ever. In some cases a monologia may be helpful, that is, a prayer consisting of just one word, a few words, or a phrase—repeated over and over again. Many times the right word or phrase will be apparent to the pastor or parishioner after some discussion about the relationship with God. At other times, traditional words such as "Jesus" or "Savior" may be used. Phrases such as the Kyrie or the Jesus Prayer ("Jesus Christ, Son of God, have mercy on me a sinner") are helpful.

Since the exhaling of breath often has a calming effect, tying in the monologia to one's breathing can sometimes be helpful. A monologia that I value is the Kyrie spoken in Greek—mentally saying "Kyrie" on the inhale and "eleison" on the exhale. Another consists of saying nothing on the inhale, and in my mind repeating "Savior" on the exhale. The Jesus Prayer can be used in similar fashion by inhaling on "Jesus Christ, Son of God" and exhaling on "have mercy on me a sinner." The use of a monologia suggests the great freedom and creativity that can be applied to one's prayer life.

It is, finally, important to remember that there are desert periods, when prayer seems nothing more than a confrontation with tightly locked steel doors that never open to our knock. Most people who have engaged in regular prayer over a large portion of their lives describe times when they do not feel like praying, or when it seems as if no one is listening. But there are other times when prayer is like a walk through the lushest rain forest—full of sights and sounds and scents that are rich in beauty and unending in variation. The pastor can help directees understand, and expect, both kinds of experience.

Scripture

Through the Bible Christians today still hear the word, as saints through the centuries have always done. Scripture can be vibrant and alive to people; it need not be an antiquated piece of parchment, as it seems to be for some. It can effectively help structure the prayer experience.

In our caring ministry we may wish to introduce a variation

of the *Lectio Divina,* assuming that clients already have
become familiar with spiritual direction and the contemplative attitude. First the directees need to quiet themselves
perhaps by way of relaxation exercises, imaging, or
regularized breathing. For those who already are fairly
relaxed, a breathing exercise done with the eyes closed can be
a good way to begin. They may count their breaths, or
mentally say, "I am," on the inhale and "calm" (or "relaxed")
on the exhale. After a few minutes they can move to using the
Jesus Prayer or some monologia, again in concert with their
breathing.

Calm, mentally receptive, and relaxed, the directees next
begin to read slowly a short passage from the Bible. They
read the same selection several times, again slowly. Usually
the pastor and parishioner have agreed in advance on the
series of scripture selections to be used. The Psalms are a
good place to begin, as is a system of readings that follows the
pattern set forth in Ignatius' description of a religious
retreat.[20] When reading the indicated portion of scripture,
directees are to reflect on the passage and listen for the word
being spoken here to them. Sometimes it is helpful to ask
simple "why" or "what" questions of the selection, that it
may begin to speak. The process should not be forced,
however; it is important to stay in the receptive mode, to
have patience, and not demand or strive for immediate,
earthshaking revelations.

The final step requires that parishioners close their eyes
and again be aware of their breathing. Now, instead of
repeating the Jesus Prayer or some monologia, they use
phrases from the given scripture selection to coordinate with
their breathing. For example, Psalm 23 (NEB) might be used,
beginning as follows:

Inhale:	The Lord is my shepherd;
Exhale:	I shall want nothing (refrain).
Inhale:	He makes me lie down in green pastures,
Exhale:	(refrain)

Inhale: [He] leads me beside the waters of peace;
Exhale: (refrain)

Inhale: He renews life within me
Exhale   (refrain).

What is actually occurring here is the formation of a prayer from those phrases of the scripture passage that seem especially compelling. It is not necessary that the directee have a photographic memory or worry about forgetting some sections. The most striking portions of the passage will in their essence be remembered, and they will become the prayer. Directees are instructed to let these remembered passages (now a prayer) speak to them—whether in feelings, images, ideas, or memories—and thus listen for the word, for God present and speaking. After having repeated these phrases for a period of time, directees are told and they come to experience that the passage continues to speak to them even after they are no longer reciting it. The speaking continues too as directees again and again reread and "pray" the scripture in the ensuring days and weeks.

Instead of being used to create a litany, scripture can find other uses too in spiritual direction. For example, after practicing some of the preparatory quieting exercises just described, directees may be asked to form an image of the biblical scene in their mind's eye. Then, after reading the passage several times, they close their eyes and, using their eyelids as a screen, they imagine themselves part of that scene—as Zacchaeus up in the tree, or as one of the lambs beside the still waters of Psalm 23. They are to smell the smells, hear the sounds, taste the food and drink. It is not necessary to move the scene's characters around as a stage director would do, but in a receptive attitude simply let happen whatever happens. Directees can also allow themselves to say or do things that are not precisely described in the passage.

The goal of such an exercise is to allow the scripture reading to come alive. Psalms, parables, and narrative sections of the Gospels are particularly appropriate for such usage. Having once visualized a passage in this way, directees can return to the same image again and again and allow it to continue to speak.

The Journal

Not all parishioners are willing to keep a journal. Some are paralyzed by a fear of writing, even though they are told that they will not have to show it to anyone, not even the pastor, and that they therefore should not concern themselves with handwriting, punctuation, neatness, syntax, or grammar. Parishioners willing to write, however, will find it beneficial to keep an ongoing journal in which they record their reflections on their own religious experience. Written reflection can give us a sense of the grace that is always operating in our life. It can foster an understanding of the patterns of grace and help us relax our striving.

Journal entries can include poetry, prose, dialogue, pictures—anything, whether spontaneous or focused. They can deal with feelings, thoughts, dreams, and intuitions; with past, present, or future. The writing should be casual in style; if it is too "well done," too full of insight, our ego becomes involved and we try energetically to make something happen rather than receptively allowing the Spirit to flow through us.

The frequency of journal entries is strictly an individual matter. For the beginner, daily entries during the first few weeks or months may be helpful for establishing the writing habit. Later entries can be more sporadic—as one is moved. The amount of time devoted to journal writing can vary from a minute to an hour, depending on the need of the moment. What has been written must not be publicly disclosed lest such disclosure damage the crucial sense of freedom needed to express oneself with complete openness and honesty.

Putting into words these feelings that overwhelm us and the images that terrorize, or inspire, us can give us perspective on what we experience. Journal writing can significantly facilitate the process of reflection in that, as Morton Kelsey states, it puts distance between self and experience. "It gives a space to deal with the cause of inner turmoil. We can bring many problems and fears into the open and deal with them face to face in honest combat. In a journal we can distinguish between friends and foes."[21] No one has done more to popularize journal writing in recent years than Ira Progoff. At his Intensive Journal Workshops he teaches people to use writing as a way of exploring their inner worlds. With a little adaptation a number of his techniques can be useful to the spiritual director.[22]

Other Disciplines

A host of other exercises can also be useful in the direction process.[23] People who have a legalistic sense of discipline may be helped by something simple and spontaneous to lighten things up. Others who are inexperienced and hungry for discipline may benefit from structure. Sometimes a focus on the body is required; where a tense and tired body blocks our attentiveness to grace, the use of yoga, sports, walking, biofeedback, or guided relaxation may be beneficial. Directors should beware, however, of touching the surface of too many disciplines without giving sustained attention to any one of them.

The Director

Regarding the spiritual director, Connolly writes:

Often, when I hear someone describe himself as a spiritual director, I picture an ageless, emaciated chap in a cowled robe, with his eyes cast down and his hands hidden in flowing sleeves. He sits in a whitewashed, cramped room with one small, barred window high on the wall beside him. Opposite him, wearing dun-colored traveling-dress and bonnet, sits a seventeenth-century French lady. Between them is a table bearing a skull and a guttered candle. She is describing the miseries of managing the family estate with her husband away at Court for much of the year. He is murmuring about being alone with the Alone, or dictating an horarium that will enable her to bring a measure of monastic order and piety into her life.[24]

One almost can smell the dusky odors of Connolly's scene, depicting as it does a hierarchical social and religious life that no longer exists. One has the impression of a spiritual director out of contact with the real world, parlaying an antiquated theology. The medieval dogma apart, just think of the connotations conveyed by the word "spiritual" to our scientific age, or the word "direction" to an age steeped in freedom and individuality. The perceptions and misperceptions people bring to spiritual direction today can make the pastor's work in this connection harder to accept than, say, psychotherapy. In the Eastern tradition the need for a guide—sage or guru—is much more widely valued.

It is obvious from the beginning that certain prerequisites are necessary for the pastor who would offer spiritual direction to late twentieth-century Christians. Pastors may already possess some of them. Others will need to be cultivated.

First, there is the skill to establish, maintain, and deepen relationships. This is a primary requirement for any pastoral carer, whether making hospital visits, offering pastoral counseling, or visiting a shut-in. The spiritual guide first befriends directees, receives them warmly, listens to them eagerly, is "with" them, and only then, in relationship, assists in their spiritual journey. People coming for direction must feel that they are loved before they can give their confidence to the director. The old image of the director as one who is uniquely "spiritual," aloof and removed from the world, holy and above sin, can hardly commend a growth process to most congregants today. Indeed, all of the interpersonal characteristics that foster effective pastoral counseling—warmth, openness, respect, listening skills, attending behaviors—are needed by the pastor who offers direction. As a directee, I must trust and respect my guide; I must know that my director hears me before I can entrust myself to the journey toward spiritual growth.

A second requirement for a pastor doing direction is an understanding of the spiritual life. As Barry and Connolly put it, "They do not need doctorates in spirituality to be competent, but they do need to have more knowledge than personal experience and common sense alone can supply."[25] Teresa of Avila and John of the Cross both emphasized this point; they railed against ignorant directors who relied only upon their own experience, knowing little of the rich tradition of spiritual practice and direction.

The knowledge required of a spiritual director includes a solid grasp of theology—an informed understanding of the faith, of spirituality, of varieties of spiritual experience and methods, and of scripture (including the tools of modern biblical scholarship). Also helpful is a base of knowledge gained from modern psychology and psychotherapy.

Seminary training in spirituality can be of great assistance. Classics such as the desert fathers and mothers, Ignatius, John of the Cross, Teresa of Avila, and Marie of the Incarnation provide rich and deep orientation. Contemporary writers such as Barry, Connolly, Edwards, Jones, Kelsey, LaPlace, Leech, May, and Merton are also useful. We need to reflect on our own prayer experience and learn from it, but we need also to relate it to that of others whom we have met or read.

A third crucial requirement for the pastor who wishes to give spiritual direction is personal religious experience. This may seem obvious, but frequently the parish demands so much of pastors that, caught up in all the activity, we have scant energy or time left for prayer and meditation. Workaholics in the parish, however, offer a negative model for other church members. They pattern a style of life that leaves little room for listening to the Spirit.

It is vital that ministers themselves experience the ebbs and flows of the Spirit's movement, the summers and winters of prayer, so that we know with confidence where hope is to be found and are persuaded that God is indeed with us—God's presence constant whether perceived by us or not. Ministers need to have faced their own fears, wrestled with their own demons, and known for themselves the undergirding love of the Christ. We require experience, and we need to have reflected on that experience.

The director should not be seen by clients as a superhuman miracle worker and problem-solver. Surely it is important that the pastor act as one in whom Christ is present, who lives daily in faith, who like Moses has spoken with God "face to face, as [one] speaks to [a] friend" (Exod. 33:11). But pastors also must communicate that we do not have special powers, a "direct line" to God, or the correct solutions for all problems. Faithful pastors have experienced the Ground of Being, to be sure, but as human beings we are still finite and fallible beings ourselves.

Many other requirements for those who would offer spiritual direction could be listed. These three seem crucial to me. But effective spiritual direction has never required ordination or a special degree. The skill for it always has been seen rather as a charism not possessed by all. Like good pastoral counselors, effective directors tend to be discovered by the Christian community. They need, in summary, skill in establishing and maintaining relationships, an understanding of the spiritual life (and of theology, psychology, and psychotherapy), and their own personal religious experience. Pastors who have these, and the charism, will be ready not only to see spiritual direction influence their care and counseling, but actually to offer spiritual direction as well.

Discernment

A final issue facing the director, already alluded to earlier, is the ability to assess growth in the directee's spiritual life—classically referred to as discernment of the Spirit. Both pastor and parishioner must decide whether the change that is occurring, and the voice they are listening to, is from God or not. Some directors have maintained that only criteria of the inner world are acceptable in making such judgments. Ignatius, however, was correct when he argued that unless a Christian is experiencing a heightened sense of God's love and unless the increased capacity to love others brings that experience into action in the world about us, spiritual exercises are not complete. Without an appropriate return to full and conscious participation in the wider community no amount of spiritual direction is fully beneficial.

How does the pastor know that an individual is growing into a deeper life in the Spirit? Although discernment is partly an intuitive matter, there are certain behaviors that give evidence to the Spirit's work. In several of his epistles Paul lists them: "But the fruit of the Spirit is love, joy, peace, patience, kindness, goodness, faithfulness, gentleness, self-control; against these there is no law" (Gal. 5:22-23).

Barry and Connolly make the point that these signs are not absolutes but always in process of development, and when their origin is indeed an action of God's Spirit they appear not sequentially but together. Patience does not make its appearance long after love and joy; it appears at least in some form along with them. "The fruits appear as unified growth, not a clutch of conflicting elements. And where there is conflict between the elements, or where one is totally lacking, the director must suspect illusion."[26] The Catholic tradition has long been suspicious of the authenticity of mystical prayer when the mystic cannot take time out to scrub pots and pans. Evidence not of how directees *think* they respond but of how they actually do respond—how they interact with others—can be immensely helpful as a gauge of how accurately they assess their inner life.

Some descriptions make it seem as if spiritual direction has reference exclusively to the inner world, but it does not. Indeed spiritual direction is not a matter of inner versus outer. It involves both. It is a movement between the two. There is a reciprocal interaction between inner life and external reality. As Jean Stairs has put it:

Our relationship with God will feed our enthusiasm to improve the quality of life around us. Prayer will clarify our vision of the world and will reflect a disposition that is willing to be critical—critical enough to be able to question the conventions and politics of our world.[27]

Our task as directors and directees alike is to listen to the inner for what our vocation (in the theological sense) should be in the outer. In this way spiritual direction serves the correlation of pastoral care and theology. If we fail to relate the two, the external world becomes a substitute for the inner world, "doing" replaces our hearing of God, and we can scarcely guess as to what God's word is for our lives. Only by listening and remaining receptive to the movements of the Spirit can we realize our true vocation and, in our finite way, be faithful to God's call.

NOTES

1. Wolfhart Pannenberg, *Christian Spirituality* (Philadelphia: Westminster Press, 1983), p. 13.

2. Don S. Browning, *The Moral Context of Pastoral Care* (Philadelphia: Westminster Press, 1976), pp. 116-30.

3. Krister Stendahl, lecture at the Association of Theological Schools Conference on Spiritual Formation, June 13, 1980.

4. C. W. Brister, *Pastoral Care in the Church* (New York: Harper & Row, 1964), p. 7.

5. David L. Fleming offers a good description of spiritual direction in his article "Models of Spiritual Direction," *Review for Religious*, 1975, pp. 351-57.

6. For a more extensive treatment the reader may wish to consult: William A. Barry and William J. Connolly, *The Practice of Spiritual Direction* (New York: Seabury Press, 1983); Tilden Edwards, *Spiritual Friend* (Mahwah, N.J.: Paulist Press, 1980); Carolyn Gratton, *Guidelines for Spiritual Direction* (Denville, N.J.: Dimension Books, 1980); Alan Jones, *Exploring Spiritual Direction: An Essay on Christian Friendship* (New York: Seabury Press, 1982); Jean LaPlace, S.J., *Preparing for Spiritual Direction* (Chicago: Franciscan Herald Press, 1975); Kenneth Leech, *Soul Friend: The Practice of Christian Spirituality* (New York: Harper & Row, 1980); Henri J. M. Nouwen, *Making All Things New: An Invitation to the Spiritual Life*, 1st ed. (New York: Harper & Row, 1981); Ira Progoff, *At a Journal Workshop* (New York: Dialog House, 1975).

7. William Barry, "Prayer in Pastoral Care," *Journal of Pastoral Care*, June, 1977, p. 94.

8. William Connolly, "Contemporary Spiritual Direction: Scope and Principles," in *Studies in the Spirituality of Jesuits* (St. Louis: American Assistancy Seminar on Jesuit Spirituality, 1975), p. 99.

9. Morton Kelsey, "Pastoral Counseling and the Spiritual Quest," *Journal of Pastoral Care*, June, 1978, p. 95.

10. William Barry and William Connolly, *The Practice of Spiritual Direction* (New York: Seabury Press, 1982), p. 11.

11. Gerald May, *Care of Mind, Care of Spirit: Psychiatric Dimensions of Spiritual Direction* (New York: Harper & Row, 1982), p. 99.

12. See especially Robert Rossi, " The Distinction Between Psychological and Religious Counseling," *Review for Religious*, 1978, pp., 546-71; Ruth Tiffany Barnhouse, "Spiritual Direction and Psychotherapy," *The Journal of Pastoral Care*, September, 1979, pp. 149-63; Tilden Edwards, *Spiritual Friend* (Mahwah, N.J.: Paulist Press, 1980), p. 130.

13. Shaun McCarty, "On Entering Spiritual Direction," *Review for Religious*, 1976, p. 858.

14. Rossi, "The Distinction Between Psychological and Religious Counseling," p. 568.

15. Howard W. Stone, *Crisis Counseling* (Philadelphia: Fortress Press, 1976).

16. Howard W. Stone, *Using Behavioral Methods in Pastoral Counseling* (Philadelphia: Fortress Press, 1980), pp. 13-30.

17. Ira Progoff, *At a Journal Workshop* (New York: Dialog House, 1977).

18. Barry, "Prayer in Pastoral Care," p. 92.

19. See Howard W. Stone, *Suicide and Grief* (Philadelphia: Fortress Press, 1972), p. 96.

20. Saint Ignacio de Loyola, *The Spiritual Exercises of St. Ignatius* (St. Louis: Institute of Jesuit Sources, 1978).

21. Morton T. Kelsey, *Adventure Inward* (Minneapolis: Augsburg, 1980), p. 25.

22. Progoff, *At a Journal Workshop*. Other useful techniques can be found in Kelsey, *Adventure Inward*.

23. Morton T. Kelsey, *The Other Side of Silence: A Guide to Christian Meditation* (Mahwah, N.J.: Paulist Press, 1976), has contributed to the field of contemporary spiritual direction through his work on meditation. He suggests five methods for meditation and gives examples of how it can be used to foster growth in the life of the Spirit. The reader who is interested in meditation is referred to Kelsey's writings on the subject.

24. Connolly, "Contemporary Spiritual Direction," p. 98.

25. Barry and Connolly, *The Practice of Spiritual Direction*, p. 131.

26. Ibid., p. 109.

27. M. Jean Stairs, *Be My Companion: A Study of Spiritual Direction* (Toronto: Image Publishing, 1982), p. 51.

6. The Priesthood of All Believers

Some churches have lately begun the practice of listing their church staff in a new way in their Sunday bulletin:

> Ministers: All the members
> of the congregation
> Pastor: The Rev. _____
> Organist: _____

The opening line may be overly cute, and affording it such priority arguable. Not to be ignored, however, is the acknowledged fact that the laity too share in the church's ministry. If prominence in the new listing can get that across, it may be worthwhile, for the fact itself surely deserves repeated emphasis, especially in our day.

Ministry and Laity

The place of the laity in the church would not have been a major issue in the church of New Testament times. Although a precise picture of what the church was like in the first century cannot be drawn, it is quite clear that there were no sharp divisions between clergy and laity.[1] Alan Richardson describes the New Testament ethos:

A layman in the New Testament sense, i.e., a member of the *laos* . . . is certainly not (as he tends to be in modern usage) a church-member who has no ministerial responsibility, one who has handed over his functions of evangelism and pastoral care to certain professional Christians who are paid to perform them. All the laity . . . if we use the term in the biblical way, are priests and ministers of the Church of Jesus Christ; and all the "ministers" are equally "laymen."[2]

This point is made dramatically in I Peter 2:9: "But you are a chosen race, a royal priesthood, a holy nation, God's own people, that you may declare the wonderful deeds of him who called you out of darkness into his marvelous light." In the original Greek the word used here for "people" is *laos*—laity. As Herman Stuempfle writes, "The people, the new race, the Christian 'folk'—without differentiation here with regard to office—were quite simply, the laity."[3]

Some differentiation between clergy and laity began to arise almost before the New Testament authors had completed their writings. Just where and when the division between them occurred is hard to document with precision, for it involved an evolutionary process. With the passage of time, however, the differentiation became increasingly pronounced—to the point where it finally became a highly controversial issue.

Vocation and Priesthood

The sixteenth-century reformers argued that ministry is not just for a special class of Christians but for all people in the church. Two theological themes that helped the Reformation churches understand ministry can also help us today. Martin Luther referred to them as (1) vocation or calling—one's station in life—and (2) implicit within it, the priesthood of all believers.

One's Station in Life

As Christians, our first calling, according to Luther, is to the state—the lot, status, station, or office—in which we find ourselves. Our vocation is not to extraordinary careers of piety, but to the common tasks that devolve upon us right where we are.

In the seventh chapter of First Corinthians Paul mentions several of these states (verses 17-24), admonishing each of his readers to "remain in the state in which he was called." We should be able to accept whatever unchangeable life situation we find ourselves in and there "lead the life which the Lord has assigned."

Luther bracketed within this first type of vocation one's occupation (as teacher, seamstress, poet, engineer, or firefighter), one's status (single, husband, wife, child), and one's place in life (rich, poor, blind, sighted). Included in our calling are thus our everyday tasks, our occupations, our studies, our daily routines. In this regard Stuempfle suggests:

Every Christian, no matter what his office or status in church or world, lived out his life under God's call . . . . Each could equally be the place of service to the neighbor, and thus to God. Luther, I think, would have liked the man who, when asked by a perfervid evangelist, "what he did to serve the Lord," responded without blinking an eye: "I bake bread."[4]

From his understanding of Paul in First Corinthians Luther argued that every station in life is equal; no one status higher than another: "The housemaid on her knees scrubbing the floor is doing a work as pleasing in the eyes of Almighty God as the priest on his knees before the altar saying the Mass."[5] We are called to perform our daily tasks as best we can, whatever the life situations in which we find ourselves, realizing that in that particular place we can perform a ministry of service to those around us.[6] Thus ministries vary according to our status in life, but all Christians, meaning specifically all laity, do minister in their particular places.

The Priesthood of All Believers

The second vocation or calling of every Christian is as a member of the priesthood of all believers. A key aspect of priesthood, since biblical times, has been the function of mediation.

Under the Mosaic covenant all the people of Israel were to be a "kingdom of priests" (Exod. 19:6 ff.; Lev. 11:44 ff.; Num. 15:40; Isa. 61:6). God is a holy God; and since human holiness is imperfect, the people of Israel needed someone to intercede for them before God. That was the function of the high priest—mediating between God and the people.

In the New Testament the terms "priesthood" and "priest" do not refer to the office of ministry. First Corinthians 12 (28 ff.) and Ephesians 4 (11 ff.) contain lists of offices and responsibilities in the church without even mentioning priests. In the New Testament there are references to only two types of Christian priesthood—the priesthood of Christ (Heb. 6:20; 7:26 ff.) and the universal priesthood (I Pet. 2:9; Rev. 5:10).

Thomas Wilkens describes with great clarity Luther's understanding of our priestly vocation:

It is a calling with, so to speak, both vertical and horizontal dimensions. Vertically, the calling grants the privilege of free access to God with the potential of faith and salvation. Horizontally, the calling occasions the responsibility of sharing the Gospel through concrete priestly functions or ministries of the Word. These are ministries of love of the first order. Yet there is another aspect of this horizontal dimension of loving ministry; that is, meeting not only one's fellow-priest with the spiritual ministries of the Word but also one's neighbor—fellow-priest or not—in love within the total context of his temporal situation and human need.[7]

In his understanding of the universal priesthood Luther recaptured much of the original biblical understanding of laity. Luther and Bucer urged the mutual cure of souls by all members of the Body of Christ. Later, pietists practiced it more widely even than during Luther's lifetime. This theme of *Seelsorge aller an allen* (the care of all for the souls of all) emphasized that the gifts of the Holy Spirit moved through all of the people of God and each had a responsibility for the mutual guidance and spiritual sustenance of the others. As John T. McNeill points out, [For Luther] "all Christians are functioning members of one living body, exercising toward one another a spiritual or priestly office."[8] Four consequences of Luther's thinking help clarify this second sense of calling:

1. The phrase "priesthood of all believers" simply advances the view that every Christian is a minister in Christ's church. Priestly functions—such as evangelism, visiting the sick and lonely, giving spiritual counsel, praying with the dying, comforting the bereaved, speaking the word of forgiveness—are not reserved for clergy. To quote Luther, "Let everyone, therefore, who knows himself to be a Christian, be assured of this, that we are all equally priests, that is to say, we have the same power in respect to the word and the sacraments."[9]

2. We are initiated into this priesthood by the washing of baptism: "Through baptism we have all been ordained as priests."[10] For each of us baptism, because it incorporates us into Christ's suffering, death, and resurrection (Rom. 6:3 ff.), marks our entrance into the community of faith. As such, it is also our induction into the universal priesthood. The soaking by water, not the donning of a stole, is what makes every Christian a minister in Christ's church.

3. The primary task of the priest is to mediate. In the Old Testament the priest stood before God and interceded for the twelve tribes. On the cross of Golgotha it was Christ, the new high priest, who stood before God and interceded for us. In the same manner we, when we mediate with our neighbor—when we go to our neighbor in love, interceding as Christ has done for us—become, as Luther puts it, "little Christs."[11] The phrase suggests not a disestablishment of priests, but an expansion of their number to include all Christians.

4. In addition to the task of mediating, there are a variety of ways in which the role of priest—minister to others—can be fulfilled. While each Christian is a member of the royal priesthood, it would lead to chaos if all were involved in the *public* preaching of the word and administration of the sacraments. For this reason the church calls and ordains certain members of the universal priesthood to serve the

functions of public ministry. Clergy and laity differ only in function; they do not constitute separate orders. Luther therefore saw the Christian, any Christian, as one who hears confessions, shares burdens, consoles, prays, listens, visits the bereaved, gives assurance of forgiveness, and performs the other tasks of ministry. Calvin required that visitation of homes be carried out not only by the pastor but also by the elders. This certainly goes beyond the usual delimitation of the laity's work today; it includes many areas that in more recent years have been reserved for clergy.

Lay Pastoral Care

Most Christians, laity and clergy alike, have no quarrel with the notion of lay ministry, whether that means involvement in acts of love toward others or a sharing in the universal priesthood of the church. But often there appears to be a discrepancy between what Christians think and what Christians do. We constantly need to be reminded of our duty as Christians. Some clergy seen reticent to recognize and encourage lay church members in doing pastoral care. And some laypersons seem paralyzed by fear when it comes to putting their faith into action in the form of a neighbor-loving pastoral care ministry.

We who preach on love of neighbor often feel judgmental when parishioners are slow to respond in ways that seem appropriate to us. Yet many of us actually inhibit laypeople from becoming priests to one another, particularly in the area of pastoral care, which we sometimes regard as our distinctively ministerial preserve.

When Sandra tells Pastor Tim about Alice being in the hospital as the result of an auto accident, Tim's first reaction is commonly: "Why is the minister always the last to know?" He feels resentful as he dashes off to the hospital. Now, that's a good thing insofar as it shows how much the pastor really cares—for Alice.

But Sandra needs care too; she needs help to grow in her own pastoral caring. Tim might have responded differently:

"Oh, Sandra, I'm sorry to hear that. How is she doing? Have you been to see her yet?" And then, affirming Sandra's visit and relating it to their *common* ministry: "Will you be able to continue visiting her? Do you think other members of the choir might want to know and visit her too? Would you be willing to get word to them?"

Sandra may have thought she was only doing a friendly thing when she visited Alice at the hospital. Pastor Tim can turn the moment of his learning about it into a teaching moment. He can help Sandra see her own priesthood, her own neighbor love, her continuing potential for pastoral care and for facilitating the care of still other parishioners.

Pastoral care is not a job for pastors only. It belongs to the whole community. It assumes—expresses and fosters—the universal priesthood. Ministry can take the form of one-on-one counseling, but it can also involve visiting, bringing in food, doing the dishes, cleaning the house, running errands, or just listening. Psychology may care for people, but a goal of pastoral care is to help people become carers themselves.

Recently in the church there has been a renewed emphasis on the pastoral care ministry of laypersons. A number of churches have teams of trained lay pastoral care visitors who call on the sick, shut-in, bereaved, and troubled. The training of laity in pastoral care methods is designed to reduce fears, enhance skills, provide methods, heighten awareness of the task, and above all to instill confidence and the conviction that even the most simple acts of caring are commissioned by God. It is a way to help parish members become active responders to God's love. It can provide an easily grasped means for unleashing their love of others within the framework of their particular status and vocation. Lay pastoral care training assists all Christians to share in the ministry to which we have all been called by the Spirit of God.[12]

Thus all Christians have two callings, two vocations. The first is to our station in life; the second is to the universal priesthood. In these callings we are to love and serve our neighbor. Pastoral care is a ministry that encompasses much of what we do for our neighbor. It is one way in which God's love is transmitted to the people about us.

NOTES

1. See Ernst Kasemann, "Paul and Early Catholicism," *New Testament Questions of Today*, trans. W. J. Montague and W. F. Bunge (Philadelphia: Fortress Press, 1969), pp. 246-47; and Herman G. Stuempfle, Jr., "Theological and Biblical Perspectives on the Laity" (pamphlet published by the Lutheran Church in America, Division for Mission in North America, 1973).

2. Alan Richardson, *An Introduction to the Theology of the New Testament* (New York: Harper & Brothers, 1959), pp. 301-2.

3. Stuempfle, "Theological and Biblical Perspectives on the Laity," p. 2.

4. Ibid., p. 6.

5. Quoted in ibid.

6. Accepting one's lot does not mean, as some have maintained, that certain people—women, Blacks, the handicapped—are therefore to be exploited and held in their place by the prevailing establishment. Each person has the responsibility to determine what can and cannot be changed.

7. Thomas G. Wilkens, "Ministry, Vocation, and Ordination: Some Perspectives from Luther," *The Lutheran Quarterly*, fall 1977, pp. 75-76.

8. John T. McNeill, *A History of the Cure of Souls* (New York: Harper & Brothers, 1951).

9. LW 36, p. 116.

10. Quoted in Paul Althaus, *The Theology of Martin Luther*, trans. Robert C. Schultz (Philadelphia: Fortress Press, 1966), p. 314.

11. Quoted in Stuempfle, "Laity," p. 4.

12. For further information on the training of laypersons in pastoral care, see Howard W. Stone, *The Caring Church: A Guide for Lay Pastoral Care* (New York: Harper & Row, 1983).

7. *Acceptance of Self and Spirit*

Rarely do I read a book in the area of mental health, pastoral counseling, or ministerial practice that does not emphasize the importance of acceptance. In these fields a clarion call over the last several decades has been: "Be accepting of others." Rogers, Carkhuff, Ivey, Clinebell, Oates, and many others have made it eminently clear that if one is to develop effective pastoral relationships one must manifest appropriate attending behaviors, careful reflective listening, suspension of judgment, and other expressions of acceptance.[1]

This call for acceptance in the interpersonal relationships of ministry is usually acknowledged and received with appropriate nods and knowing smiles. I have often sounded the same call myself.[2] Who could possibly disagree? Who indeed could possibly favor nonacceptance, rejection, a therapeutic cold shoulder? In fact, the acceptance of acceptance is now so common as to deserve fresh reflection and critique.

Acceptance

Recently while listening to a lecture on pastoral counseling in the parish, I heard again the familiar call: "The key to doing good pastoral counseling is that you really accept persons." The comment from the podium triggered for me a reflective detour. What did the speaker really mean when he made that assertion? What did he understand "acceptance" to be?

Tuning in to the lecturer once again, I soon began to get a clearer picture of his meaning: Acceptance requires the carer to value, to listen carefully, and to believe in and work with individuals in spite of what they have or have not done. No conditions for such acceptance can be laid out in advance. Acceptance is not something awarded to people only after they have "cleaned up their act." Nor is it grounded in their prior subscription to a particular code of ethics. The speaker was clearly advising me to just accept people as they are, in spite of what they have done or not done. I half expected to hear strains of "Just As I Am" in the background; instead of a hymn, however, there flowed quotations from Carl Rogers and other psychotherapists to buttress the point. Only belatedly, almost as an afterthought, did the lecturer also refer to theologian Paul Tillich's sermon "You Are Accepted."[3]

Now there are good reasons for stressing the importance of acceptance in pastoral care. The emphasis represents a legitimate correction of certain historic, and even contemporary, forms of ministry in which the approach to others often conveyed an almost overbearing parental attitude: You must do what God wills (meaning, "as I say"). In reality, few of the choices we face in life are simple, clear-cut, black-and-white choices; most fall into various shades of gray. Furthermore, our situation today is marked by a radically changed attitude toward authority: *Herr Pastor* is out, "Pastor Bill" is in. Our attending and listening to parishioners are valued, but our telling them what to do is not, because most people prefer to discover the answers for themselves.

I personally have experienced acceptance by another and been grateful for it. Probably nothing has a more powerful influence on your life than to know that someone is *for* you—through thick and thin, whether you act appropriately or not. Such acceptance serves as a center, a home base out of which all of life can flow. Its absence in some cases can generate a frantic drive to gain acceptance by any means possible and at whatever cost; it can even lead to the lethargy of depressive seclusion as we anxiously seal ourselves off from others. The speaker who recently triggered my reflection was surely correct in asserting that acceptance is a key component in pastoral care. Nonetheless I for one still find the notion a bit unsettling.

My uneasiness perhaps arises from the way in which unconditional acceptance is often meted out in actual practice. As applied, our acceptance of people as they are rarely seems to include any valuing of the transcendent, any reverence for spirit.[4] For those who are theologically concerned about pastoral care this should give pause.

Rather than simply adopting wholesale the sound psychotherapeutic principle of acceptance, we need to examine carefully its meaning and to broaden our understanding of it to the point where persons are accepted not only as they *are* but also as they can *become* in the life of the Spirit. We dare not assume that an "as is" acceptance on our part will naturally and as a matter of course lead someone to transcend self[5] for life in the Spirit—experience simply does not bear out such an easy assumption. We need instead to take a fresh and hard look at acceptance, particularly as it relates to our understanding of self and spirit.

Self and Spirit

The "self" is the organizing center of human response and activity within each of us. Rogers thinks of self as that "organized consistent conceptual gestalt" which is composed of various perceptions of the "I" or "me" in relation to the world and other people, and the values that are placed on these perceptions.[6] This self has been variously designated as ego, soul, heart, or "I." But whatever the name, the reference is clearly to the locus of perception, organization, decision making, and response. The self is the internal regulatory system of human mentation and activity.

In most forms of psychotherapy and pastoral care the purpose of counseling is to strengthen the self. Expressions such as "weak ego-strength" or "lack of self-esteem," technically not synonymous, are typically used by mental health professionals to describe an individual with a weak or undeveloped self. Although psychological approaches to treatment are diverse in the way they describe their goals, most do focus on this center of organization, and their purpose is to strengthen the self and foster some form of self-actualization.

The "spirit" on the other hand is that facet of the individual wherein God is most directly encountered. "It is the Spirit himself bearing witness with our spirit that we are children of God" (Rom. 8:16). In the Bible "spirit" (usually *pneuma* in the New Testament and *ruach* in the Old Testament) is used variously to describe God, incorporeal beings, manifestations of God, and the divine power in human beings.[7] This last understanding is the one that concerns us here.

Ernst Kasemann believes that of all the New Testament writers Paul has the only "thoroughly thought-out doctrine" of person.[8] Pastoral care, then, should be expected to take the Pauline understanding seriously, for it is in Paul's doctrine of person that the significance of spirit is made prominent. For Paul the term "spirit" designates the new power, summoning to faith, that comes to Christians in their rebirth. In Galatians 2:20 he characterizes their new situation: "It is no longer I who live, but Christ who lives in me." Baptism marks the death of the old person and the beginning of new life which is grounded in the resurrection.

Reinhold Niebuhr in discussing the self/spirit distinction maintains that in the New Testament "the Hebraic sense of the unity of body and soul is not destroyed while, on the other hand, spirit is conceived of as primarily a capacity for and affinity with the divine."[9]

For Paul spirit means the entire being as it is physically and spiritually related to God as the center of identity. Spirit is not a repudiation of the flesh (appetites and emotions) but a centering of them and all else in God. Eduard Schweizer puts it this way:

Paul thinks wholly in terms of the work of the Spirit of God and perceives that the whole existence of the believer is determined thereby. For Paul the Spirit of God is not an odd power which works magically; the Spirit reveals to the believer God's saving work in Christ and makes possible his understanding and responsible acceptance thereof. For this reason the pneuma, though always God's Spirit and never evaporating into the pneuma given individually to man, is also the innermost ego of the one who no longer lives by his own being but by God's being for him.[10]

Paul invites Christians to an existence that is responsive to the summons of the Spirit. His call is for an attentive openness to the Spirit whereby believers allow their selves to be molded by God (Rom. 8:6, 14; Gal. 5:16). Life in the Spirit means a self that is oriented body and soul to God, an identity that is centered in God. "Spirit" has reference not to a portion of me but to all that I am, my whole being, as focused on hearing and responding to the word.

The self as organizing center for a person's activity tends to respond to the individual's needs, drives, wants, cognitions, and perceptions of reality. It has difficulty looking beyond these primary stimuli. But when the spirit is attentive to God, transcendence of self becomes possible because self is now centered in the word.

Self is not necessarily identical to spirit. The spirit's task is to transform the self into a likeness of Christ (Rom. 8:29). The spirit presupposes and works with the abilities and attributes we have and enhances them; it does not negate the structures of selfhood but provides them with a capacity that they hitherto lacked, namely, a certain possibility for life in God's Spirit. The change that occurs when God's Spirit resides in human spirit is always an eschatological change—an "already now but not yet." The power of the self remains in tension with that of the spirit.

Self and spirit become identical only when spirit fully apprehends the self. As John Cobb writes, "The self is spirit only when the self as the organizing center transcends the emotions and other aspects of the psychic life."[11] Only as self takes responsibility for one's whole life, and orients it in its entirety to the word, do self and spirit coalesce.

Two Forms of Acceptance

The "as is" acceptance so common in psychotherapy has reference to self, not spirit. What is appropriate in psychological counseling, however, may not be sufficient for the ministry of pastoral care. Psychotherapy's "as is" acceptance has raised a whole range of theological concerns. It contains no ethical components; for example, it allows one to listen primarily to one's own needs and desires rather than to the word of God; it relies on a limited kind of acceptance (by the carer) while ignoring the only complete and perfect acceptance (that which comes from God); and it tends to turn one's attention more inward (toward self) than outward (toward neighbor). Our major concern here, however, has to do with the fact that "as is" acceptance typically does not recognize spirit and hence is not responsive to God's call for a life in the Spirit.

Diana Wing, a young and intelligent management trainee, was overwhelmed with doubts about her own capabilities. Psychotherapy assisted her to overcome these doubts and to appraise her skills and abilities more realistically, but it did not address the "winning is everything" ethos that shaped her life in both job and family. In fact her therapist's nonjudgmental acceptance, by neglecting review of these ethical values, was tantamount to an affirmation of them. Therapeutic acceptance tended to deny to Diana the possibility of transcending self and of extending love beyond self. While, for her, self was indeed strengthened, spirit was not. Although she now feels better, functions more effectively on her job, and is more realistic about herself—all good things, to be sure—there is no movement toward a new life informed by the spirit.

Acceptance in pastoral care values both self and spirit. It not only affirms the person who *is* but also appreciates who that person can *become* in Christ. Pastoral acceptance of this sort exists in an ongoing tension between the desires of the self and the summons of the spirit, between the "as is" of the present and the lure or call forward of the future (as some process theologians have described the invitation of the Spirit of God).[12]

This call forward, as it is played out in the minister's acceptance of others, is significantly different from a parental no-no, a scripture-quoting condemnation, or a conditional

"I'll accept you when you shape up." It is actually a more complete kind of acceptance in that it not only recognizes present realities but also has a vision of future possibilities in the Spirit. It maintains that who we *really* are is far more than what we are just *now*. We have not yet received or incorporated all that God has to give; nor have we wholly apprehended God's intention or mission for us. The Spirit compels us to look toward Jesus as a pattern for what we are *becoming* and thus to know what by God's grace we *truly* are. Theologically responsible acceptance in pastoral care is eschatological to the core.

Acceptance in Pastoral Care

The pastoral care that functions out of an acceptance of self *and* spirit is likely to differ in significant ways from the psychotherapy or pastoral counseling that proceeds on the basis of "as is" acceptance. There are concrete ways in which ministers can work to incorporate both self and spirit in their pastoral acceptance. Four areas are worth immediate mention: refocusing the pastor's perspective to more fully include spirit; restructuring care methods to more completely address spirit; speaking to issues of spirit during the care process; and revitalizing the minister's own personal openness to spirit.

Perspective will surely be a key characteristic distinguishing the ministerial counselor from the psychologist.[13] How the pastor views a person's plight and rescue will significantly affect the care offered. From the very beginning, ministers with an understanding of self/spirit acceptance will look and listen for the subtle movements of spirit betokened by the other person's words. We cannot assume that people respond only out of their own needs or wants, drives or compulsions; we will instead recognize each faint hint of aspirations that may lead to transcendence of self. We may, for example, discern (and comment on) a parishioner's impulse to love others that goes beyond any personal assessment of (physical or psychic) attractiveness and approaches a kind of selfless or unselfish love. As pastors we can try to refocus our perspective, and that of the people we serve, to include spirit as well as self.

A second way to broaden pastoral acceptance is to recognize that, in self/spirit acceptance, care of spirit is at least as important as actualization of self. As a result of such recognition, our methods of care may well begin to take on aspects of spiritual direction (which aims at strengthening the relationship with God) while relying less exclusively on aspects of psychological counseling, which tends primarily to address problems of self. In addition, we will not assume, as much pastoral counseling still does, that self must be responded to *prior to* spirit. Each is a legitimate area of counseling concern, each a possible starting point for care. In fact, pastoral care best addresses both areas—the whole person—at once rather than concentrating on either one to the exclusion of the other. There is always the danger that where issues of self are more recognizable, and obviously pressing to the parishioner, they will easily take first priority, and sometimes become the only issue addressed. To deal with spirit only "as time permits," however, often means in practice to ignore spirit altogether.

A third way of broadening pastoral experience so that it includes both self and spirit is to recall that the Spirit's revelation occurs as the word of God is embodied. God is revealed in both spoken and visible form. The word of God is expressed both verbally (in preaching, teaching, scripture reading, and other written and spoken sharing of the message of Christ) and visibly (in the sacraments, an icon, Brahms' *Requiem*, an embrace, a listening ear, a warm smile, the sign of the cross, a meal brought to the mourners' home, one's ministry of presence). (See chapter 3.) Pastoral care must be alert to this twofold address of the word. God communicates and establishes relationship with God's people in both ways, and pastoral care needs to emphasize both in the help it offers.

In pastoral care the word is made manifest or visible in the dignity and respect with which the pastor treats the person. The finite worth of the individual is articulated not only in

what is said but also in the *way* things are said and in the way
the person is treated. Pastors accept the person *and* act out
that acceptance, valuing not only who that person is now but
also who that person can become in the unfolding of the
spirit.

The verbal word is proclaimed in that moment of the care
process when the minister helps interpret what the
unfolding of spirit could mean for the person. As rapport is
established and a relationship develops, there will come
times when the minister can speak prophetically—not only
expressing love "as is" but also helping the person discover
what life in the Spirit can be. As Cobb has pointed out, there
is a difference between desires and aspirations: "We *desire* to
gain ends that are set by our emotions. But our spiritual
aspirations are for the change of our desires. . . . They deal
with the motivations of our actions. For example, we may
aspire to become people who act out of disinterested love for
others rather than out of emotional desires.

"Such disinterested love is possible in principle only at the
level of spirit."[14]

Pastoral care speaks to people concerning this difference
between desires and aspirations in order that self can be
informed by spirit in the decisions that are faced. The
prophetic and interpretive components of ministry are
integral to pastoral care in which the minister verbally
encourages individuals in their openness to spirit and their
aspirations of disinterested love.

Finally, in the realities of parish life these prophetic and
interpretive insights may be hard to come by. Scurrying
about from meetings to appointments, worried about
newsletter deadlines, sermon preparation, negative cash
flow, and people's urgent cries for help, it is easy to be caught
up—no, it is hard *not* to be caught up—in so many activities
and demands that one's *own* spirit is ignored. Pastoral care
that is open to spirit requires a minister who is open to spirit,
who is not so dragged down by a myriad of activities as to
have no time left for quiet listening and prayer. Only through
a disciplined, daily, open attentiveness to God's voice is one
enabled to sense the sometimes ever-so-slight stirrings of

spirit in one's own life and in the lives of others. It is difficult to share with others our insights and directives about spirit when our own spirit is tranquilized by inactivity.

Acceptance in pastoral care is thus broader than acceptance in psychotherapy, which also has a concern for the wholeness of persons. The wholeness to which pastoral care ministry aspires requires that the minister accept both self and spirit. Pastoral acceptance that recognizes only the self ("as is" acceptance) and does not value the call of spirit is inadequate, for the fundamental goal of the Christian is a life in the Spirit of Christ. Ministers who would assist others to be attentive to the Spirit's call must themselves be attentive to the Spirit *and* accept others not merely as they are now but as they can be, as they are becoming, as God intends them to be.

NOTES

1. See Robert Carkhuff, *Helping and Human Relations*, vol. 1 (New York: Holt, Rinehart & Winston, 1969), pp. 46-145; Howard Clinebell, *Basic Types of Pastoral Counseling* (Nashville: Abingdon Press, 1966), pp. 27-94; Gerard Egan, *The Skilled Helper*, 2nd ed. (Monterey, Calif.: Brooks/Cole Publishing Co., 1982), pp. 32-147; Carl R. Rogers, *Client Centered Therapy* (Boston: Houghton Mifflin Co., 1951).

2. See especially this author's books *Crisis Counseling* and *The Caring Church*.

3. Paul Tillich, *The Shaking of the Foundations* (New York: Charles Scribner's Sons, 1948), pp. 153-63.

4. Carl R. Rogers probably has done the most theoretically to define acceptance for psychological counseling. Acceptance or "unconditional positive regard" he describes as "a warm, positive and acceptant attitude toward what *is* in the client. . . . It involves the therapist's genuine willingness for the client to be whatever feeling is going on in him at that moment—fear, confusion, pain, pride, anger, hatred, love, courage, or awe. . . . He does not simply accept the client when he is behaving in certain ways, and disapprove of him when he behaves in other ways. It means an ongoing positive feeling without reservations, without evaluations." *On Becoming a Person* (Boston: Houghton Mifflin Co., 1961), p. 62.

5. To "transcend self" here means to perceive the self accurately and take responsibility for it, as well as to lose oneself in commitment to the greater concerns of the larger group.

6. Carl Rogers quoted in C. H. Patterson, *Theories of Counseling and Psychotherapy* (New York: Harper & Row, 1966), p. 407.

7. S. V. McCasland, "Spirit," in *The Interpreter's Dictionary of the Bible*, vol. IV, ed. George A. Buttrick (Nashville: Abingdon Press, 1962), pp. 432-34.

8. Ernst Kasemann, *Perspectives on Paul* (Philadelphia: Fortress Press, 1971), pp. 1-2.

9. Reinhold Niebuhr, *The Nature and Destiny of Man*, vol. 1 (New York: Charles Scribner's Sons, 1949), p. 152.

10. Eduard Schweizer, "Spirit," in *Theological Dictionary of the New Testament*, vol. 6, ed. Gerhard Friedrich, trans. Geoffrey W. Bromiley (Grand Rapids: William B. Eerdmans, 1968), p. 436.

11. John B. Cobb, Jr., *Theology and Pastoral Care* (Philadelphia: Fortress Press, 1977), p. 12.

12. See John B. Cobb, Jr., *The Structure of Christian Existence* (Philadelphia: Westminster Press, 1967) and *God and the World* (Philadelphia: Westminster Press, 1969); see also Gordon E. Jackson, *Pastoral Care and Process Theology* (Washington, D.C.: University Press of America, 1981).

13. See pp. 30-31.

14. Cobb, *Theology and Pastoral Care*, p. 16.

8. Suffering

Like several other graduate student families nearing the end of their stay at Claremont, my wife, Karen, and I decided to have a child. I had completed my comprehensive exams and the dissertation was coming alone nicely. Underfoot already was a five-year-old, and if ever we were to have a second child, this was the time.

Karen was in excellent health, and the first half of her pregnancy went smoothly. She had just begun wearing her old corduroy maternity clothes when the problems began. At the time, I did not understand completely what the obstetrician had to say, but one phrase came through clearly: "I'm not sure the fetus is developing as it should."

The next few weeks were a time of anxiety and waiting. Finally, the word came: "The fetus is dead." Period. The doctor did not know what went wrong; he could only surmise that "the fetus was abnormal in some way and would most likely have been born with defects, or worse."

For several more weeks Karen carried our loss around with her, literally. Finally, in a middle-of-the-night emergency operation six months after conception, the remaining tissue was removed along with our dreams for this dearly wanted child.

The doctor was perfunctory. "Wait six months to a year and you can try again," he cheerfully advised. To him we had lost a fetus; to us, it was the baby we had put off having, the one who was never to be. I was not interested in some future possibility. (Today, the five-year-old who was underfoot back in 1970 is still our only child.)

Miscarriages are difficult enough to accept in the first month or so of pregnancy, but we had begun to think of this baby as part of our family. Karen had started feeling, as she drove around town on errands, that she was not alone—that she had brought that other person along with her.

The response of our family and friends was overwhelming. They rallied around, expressed their love, cleaned and cooked and listened. Still we grieved.

Why did this happen? How could a loving God allow this? If God is all good and all powerful, why did God let this occur? Where is God when I need God? *Why?*

I was too "sophisticated" theologically to voice any of these questions out loud. Nevertheless, I secretly wondered about a God who had promised always to be with us, but did not seem to be around just when we needed God. I never voiced those questions to anyone, and no one broached the issue of theodicy with either of us. I did talk to friends about the pain in my heart, but I also would have liked to talk about the whys ricocheting in my head.

The loss of our wished-for child led me to much reflection and to reading books that addressed my questions. The question of "theodicy"—the justification of God's righteousness in the face of so much implausible evil and suffering—has been posed by many thoughtful people in every age. Yet it continues to be the Gordian Knot of monotheism, and a hard problem for all who proclaim such faith. We ministers need to shape both our theological understanding of the issue and our approach to addressing it in the concrete situations of pastoral care.

Toward a Theology of Theodicy

In any context, one asks about the why of suffering with great trepidation, knowing that whatever we say will at best be only partially adequate. Yet address the question we must, since theodicy is one of the most important theological issues affecting pastoral care: "No profession faces the direct question of the meaning of suffering more frequently than ministry," says Thomas Oden. "And no theological dimension of the pastor's work is more difficult. Theodicy remains among the most perplexing, practically pressing, and difficult of the theological issues of pastoral practice. Ultimately, it affects every other dimension in one's ministry."[1]

In the seminary environment where I teach, I discovered that students discussing pastoral cases or reviewing video tapes of counseling sessions invariably find it difficult to respond to the issue of seemingly needless suffering. They view on tape a person in severe pain, dying of cancer, and then I challenge them: "Now assume that you are there actively listening, showing acceptance. How would you respond?" The replies are almost predictable: " I don't know what to say," "I don't have anything to say." At first I thought that my students were inarticulate in such situations because they were new and inexperienced in the field of pastoral care. But then I began to examine how I myself respond to the why questions and I discovered that I had a repertoire of fairly safe ways for ignoring them or changing the subject. We all know the paralysis experienced in the face of such a frightening, and sometimes devastating, topic.

From other pastoral counselors and from seminary colleagues, however, I was able to receive much help for my own reflections on theodicy as a pastoral counseling issue. The reflections presented here on suffering in a Christian context will focus primarily on the personal suffering most commonly encountered in pastoral care, those connected with such events as death, divorce, job loss, disability, and terminal illness. This is not to gainsay the Christian concern for societal and global suffering, but only to focus and limit the present chapter. In addition many interpretations of suffering ignore the distinction between the suffering we can end and that which we cannot. We will speak here only of the latter, the suffering that arises out of inevitable or irreversible events that do not readily yield to social, political, medical, or even charitable solutions.

The attempt in this chapter is not to recapitulate the variety of theories concerning theodicy, but rather to put forward some ideas that have been helpful for me in shaping my own understanding of it.[2] In these few pages I will construct the skeleton of a theology of theodicy that I hope will assist readers in further shaping their own theological viewpoint.

The New Testament offers no formal theodicy except for the eschatological reassurance that for the faithful "all things work together for good" (Rom. 8:28 KJV). Yet, as Langdon Gilkey points out, "For many sincere Christians, both the intellectual question of evil and vivid personal experiences of evil, in war and disease, in sin and death, have done more to shake their faith in God than anything else."[3] Indeed, most of us do not even think much about theodicy—except in the midst of suffering, at a point when dispassionate exploration and reflection is nearly impossible, because we are in much pain or are called to serve someone in pain. Even then people, like myself, may not raise the question out loud, How can God allow such a tragedy? but they will ponder it, trying to make sense of the perceived incongruities.

The question confronts us with several major issues. If God is both loving and all-powerful, how can evil exist? What is the distinction between moral and natural evil? Do humans cause all evil, or just moral evil? Is God's relationship to creation a close one emphasizing active involvement or a loose one emphasizing human freedom? What effect does the Cross, our redemption, have on an understanding of suffering? Finally, is suffering necessary in order for one to be Christian?

God as Both Loving and All-powerful

First, the basic problem of theodicy is this: *either* God is all-powerful but refuses to abolish evil (and therefore is not loving), or God is loving but unable to abolish evil (and therefore is not all-powerful). Three variables exist here: God is love, God is all-powerful, evil exists. The problem is that Christian faith affirms what all reason and logic deny—the concurrent validity of all three.

Now if there is no God, the solution is easy: We simply say the world is evil. Then, responding to people in suffering, we do not have to ask why—that's just the way it is.

For twentieth-century Christians who believe in God, the easiest way to resolve the problem may be to view God not as all-powerful, but as one who after creating the world stands back from creation and does not presently govern it. Such a view assumes that God has little or nothing to do with the course of events. A difficulty with this position, however, is that the scriptures witness to a God of history; Christianity is unique in its emphasis on the incarnation, on God active in history, bringing us redemption.

Another possible solution to the theodicy problem is to deny the all-loving quality of God. Even to conceive of God as unloving, however, or uncaring, would be difficult for any contemporary Christian. Alternatively, there is the interpretation that conceives of evil in the world as not being *really* evil; "bad" events being somehow God's will, are not *really* bad. Our suspicions of this position are buttressed every day; as we read the paper or watch the newscasts it is difficult to hold that the events being reported are unequivocally good. Besides, if evil were not real, would we have the Cross?

God the Creator

To try to resolve this apparent contradiction—an all-powerful and all-loving God coexisting with evil—we must look at God's relationship to creation. To what extent is God involved in all that happens around us and to us? How active, or removed, is God?

One view sees God as actively involved in creation: God is the primary cause of everything that occurs. God is involved in the skinning of my knee. The things that happen, happen because they are God's will—hurricanes, flowers, birth, death, and my skinned knee. If I need plane fare to visit my ailing grandmother and I pray about it, then when the money turns up, God's hand has been in it; it is an answer to prayer. The danger in such a view is that it can lead to human attempts to manipulate God. On the positive side, though, such a view does allow for petitionary prayer; I can pray for material things and even for the healing of someone who is ill, since God is intimately involved in all that happens. This view of God's active involvement strongly emphasizes the immanence of God.

But there is also the view that sees God as removed from the world: I skin my knee, not by God's design or will, but by my own foolhardiness in not looking where I was going. God is not active in everything, or anything, that occurs. Pushed to its extreme, this is the position of Deism, in which God "the clockmaker" wound up the world and then withdrew to let it tick away unattended. This view acknowledges that people get cancer because of the multiplying of bad cells; hurricanes are spawned by winds interacting with one another.

An advantage of this view is that it does not lay evil at God's doorstep; evil occurs because of natural causes or because of our misuse of freedom. This view of God's aloofness strongly emphasizes God's transcendence. A disadvantage is that prayer as a consequence, effects little more than psychological side benefits; it can bring me peace perhaps, or inner strength, or calm the storm within, but there is no use praying for divine intervention. I can ask God to be with those who are ill, but I cannot ask for their healing, except as God would allow the physicians to use their natural talents.[4]

In terms of Christian theology there is no definitive answer to the question of God's involvement or lack of involvement in the world. Cogent arguments can be made for both positions. My personal view is closer to the second than to the first, though with a stronger sense of God's continuing agency in the world. A view of a God as being only loosely tied to creation is helpful for the modern mind because it embodies a firmer understanding of natural causation within the world.

When someone asked Jesus why a certain man was born blind, Jesus turned the question aside and then healed the man; God's will is not directly linked to everything that happens. However, I do not believe we can support the view of an impotent God; rather God freely chooses to limit God's power in order to allow humans freedom of action, without which there can be no real love. But God can alter God's choice at any time; God can, and does, act not only in creation and incarnation, but also in our lives. On this view prayer becomes a way to hear God's word for us, and petitionary prayer has a central place in pastoral care: God is still the God of history.

The Problem of Evil

It seems to me that, however fancy our theological footwork, evil cannot be denied. Classically, theologians have spoken of two types of evil—natural evil and moral evil. By natural evil they mean that all things are created intrinsically good, yet can themselves be the cause of immense devastation and suffering. For example, winds can lead to hurricanes; growth, to cancer; water, to floods; and fire, to destruction. God is not the cause of such natural evil; God only allows it.[5] In other words, God is the basis of the possibility for evil in creation, though not its cause. So far as natural evil is concerned, God is removed from the world. God can and does intervene in the natural order of things, but only occasionally, as an exception to the rule, for in the creation God deliberately limited God's self, allowing natural processes such as winds and growth, hurricanes and cancer, to occur as they do. Contemporary Christians, therefore, generally do not place religious significance on a specific calamity or illness; natural evil is absurd, that is, without explanation, and to blame it on God would be ludicrous, however much insurance companies may refer to such losses as "acts of God."

It is interesting that the Gospels never speak of God expunging natural evil from human existence; instead they address questions of moral evil.[6] By moral evil theologians have traditionally meant that evil which results from the misuse of human freedom, that freedom with which we are created as beings separate from God. It is called "sin." This is what Paul writes so much about in his letters to the early Christian churches. He sees each person as having free choice, and in the exercise of that freedom making actual choices that lead away from God. There can be no freedom at all, without the freedom to say no to God. Murder, child abuse, rape—all are examples of how humans misuse their freedom and cause suffering. Every day millions of people, created in the image of God, are acting and reacting to their physical environment and to other people. Out of these interactions, or lack thereof, evil erupts and widespread suffering results, and the world, created good, is jolted by its consequences, indeed may someday be annihilated by them.

Thus, God is surely omnipotent and loving, but limits God's self, out of love, both in relationship to nature and in relationship to human freedom. As creator, God is the *basis* for all that happens, both good and evil, but not its *cause*. As part of the created world, humans are participants in its beauty and goodness, but also subject to its ugliness and suffering; as free agents we are contributors to both.

The Tension of Faith

How then do we understand the why questions, the issue of theodicy, the cause and meaning of suffering? There is no clear answer. The New Testament's answer is essentially wait and see. Not much help to many of us today perhaps, but there it is.

Søren Kierkegaard stresses that, to make sense of suffering, a transition is required from scientific thinking to the religious mode of belief and faith. When most people ask why, they are asking scientific rather than religious questions. We seek root causes. Most of us would of course deny that we can use scientific methods to prove the existence of God; yet we forget that when we ask why questions in the face of suffering we are actually employing scientific cause-and-effect thinking.[7] Kierkegaard writes:

But that the heavy suffering is good is something that must be *believed*, because it cannot be seen. Perhaps we can see afterwards that it *has been* good, but at the time of suffering we can neither see it, nor, even though ever so many people with the best of motives keep on repeating it, can we hear it spoken; it must be believed. It is the thought of faith we need, and the earnest, confident, frequent expressing of this thought to ourselves. . . . But when one looks on unmixed misery all around, then by faith to see the joy: yea, this is meet and proper. It is meet and proper so to speak of faith, for faith is always the reference to what is not seen, whether the *invisible* or the *improbable*.[8]

So the Christian in the midst of suffering is compelled to ask why because faith insists on holding together in irreconcilable tension three things that logically do not stand together: God is love, God is all-powerful, and evil exists.

It is right and proper for believers to raise questions of theodicy, to wonder about suffering as the ending of the book of Job implies. Ultimately, though, all analogies and metaphors fail. The choice God made in creating the world the way it is, and in continuing to respond to it the way God has, is beyond our human conception. This does not mean that we should not try to understand it, or that we should cease asking questions; it means only that our quest will never be finally successful. Our answers will always be tentative, our perspective finite. The resolution to our despair and anger will have to take the form not of an intellectual conclusion but of a renewal in faith, hope, and love. Indeed, just when Job sulks, screams, and pleads with God for an answer to the why, he does not get one—at least not the answer he expects. For God does not give a defensible answer that could be reviewed and critiqued academically. Instead, God replies, in effect: "Job, who do you think you are? You can't know. You can't judge what is best, only I can. You're a human and I am God, and that is the difference of night and day." The question is not really answered but Job nonetheless rests in the answer, for he is not God; he cannot view things from God's vantage point. Only in faith can we understand—and then only in a very limited way.

Emil Brunner speaks of people who do not believe when

they suffer; they too feel sure that they are innocent and that their suffering is undeserved. Then he makes the point:

Indeed, the theodicy problem finally proves to be a form of unbelief, in so far as man allows himself to adopt the role of an objective neutral spectator, in so far, that is, as the question is raised from a point outside one's own responsibility, according to the connexion between the will of God and the evil in the world.[9]

Suffering, he concludes, can finally be understood only in light of the Cross.

God the Redeemer

If the question of theodicy is not answered as we might have hoped, what is God's response? God's answer is Christ. Not only is God the creator who limits God's self; God is also the redeemer who enters life as a sharer in our suffering. God does not remain aloof. God is intensely engaged, suffers, and is the first to enter into the resurrection. Incarnation and crucifixion are not so much an answer to the question as they are a redefinition of the world, and of our relationship to God in it, such that the question itself comes to mean something different.

Elie Wiesel, a survivor of the Holocaust, was brought to Auschwitz when he was not quite fifteen years old. In his book *Night* he recalls how the experience devastated his once deep faith:

Never shall I forget that night, the first night in camp, which has turned my life into one long night, seven times cursed and seven times sealed. Never shall I forget that smoke. Never shall I forget the little faces of the children, whose bodies I saw turned into wreaths of smoke beneath a silent blue sky.
Never shall I forget those flames which consumed my faith forever.[10]

Wiesel writes of being forced to witness the execution by hanging of three people—two men and a young boy who he said had a face like a sad angel.

"Long live liberty!" cried the two adults.

But the child was silent.

"Where is God? Where is He?" someone behind me asked. . . .

The two adults were no longer alive. . . . But the third rope was still moving; being so light, the child was still alive.

For more than half an hour he stayed there, struggling between life and death, dying in slow agony under our eyes. . . .

Behind me, I heard the same man asking:

"Where is God now?"

And I heard a voice within me answer him:

"Where is He? Here He is—He is hanging here on this gallows."[11]

Francois Mauriac talked with Wiesel about the experience while Wiesel was still a young man, working as a journalist in Paris. In the Foreword to *Night* Mauriac writes of their talk:

And I, who believe that God is love, what answer could I give my young questioner, whose dark eyes still held the reflection of that angelic sadness which had appeared one day upon the face of the hanged child? What did I say to him? Did I speak of that other Jew, his brother, who may have resembled him—the Crucified, whose Cross has conquered the world? Did I affirm that the stumbling block to his faith was the cornerstone of mine, and that the conformity between the Cross and the suffering of men was in my eyes the key to that impenetrable mystery whereon the faith of his childhood had perished? . . . We do not know the worth of one single drop of blood, one single tear. All is grace. If the Eternal is the Eternal, the last word for each one of us belongs to Him. This is what I should have told this Jewish child. But I could only embrace him, weeping.[12]

Jewish thought does, in fact, view God in God's empty and debased form as sharing the torment of people in exile, in prison, in martyrdom. This is implied in the Hebrew understanding of *shekinah*—the "indwelling presence of God in the world"; God suffers wherever people suffer.

As Christians, we see in Christ's suffering and death on the cross God's response to the question, "Did God create evil?" God did not create evil (although certainly the possibility for it), but endures it along with us. God is not the hangman, not a spectator—an aloof deity; but rather God suffers, and through Christ is with us in our suffering. The gospel is that in Christ we are saved not only *out of* our suffering, but also *through it*. This is not to say that God is concerned only for the broken and undone; surely God is concerned also for health, happiness, and a good quality of life. But in suffering, which is inevitable, we are united with the Christ. There is one who has gone before us, not in power and strength but in weakness, humbled and abused. In the pain and isolation of Jesus' cry, "My God, my God, why have you forsaken me?" he becomes one with us.

A resurrected god who rose from the dead after dying peacefully in his bed of old age, without any suffering whatever, would be a different divinity from the Christ. What comes after always somehow includes what went before. At no point can you ever be as though you had not experienced the previous years of your life. One can be forgiven all that has gone before, but one can never erase it. The same is true of the resurrection; it does not cancel the death that preceded it. After the resurrection, Jesus bore in his hands and sides the marks of his violent death. Still today he carries them, and the suffering, transformed but not canceled.

So, even though we may picture God the Creator as somehow more removed from the world than actively involved in its day-to-day affairs, in God the Redeemer we see a different picture—of a God who walks with us along our lonely paths. The gospel does not picture God as the totally other depicted in the creation story; instead it shows Christ as the totally involved one who suffers beatings, abuse, hunger, thirst, pain, loneliness, and finally a death in which he is seemingly forsaken by God.

The Greeks believed that if a god suffered—and even love was a suffering kind of passion—its perfection was negated. But according to New Testament faith it is in God's very suffering and subsequent resurrection that God's perfection is made evident. In the case of Jesus, God's perfection was revealed, not negated, by the scandal of the passion. To the amazement of disciples and enemies alike, God's power manifested itself in Jesus' self-giving love, in weakness and vulnerability. Gilkey writes, "Truly here was one of the most radical transformations of values in all historical experience: not the avoidance of suffering, but its willing acceptance in love, became the deepest clue to divinity."[13]

Many people who have experienced suffering have done so without knowing God as the one who suffers. They may have looked to God for power and strength and miracles, but not for this! The school of suffering, however, requires meeting the Savior where he is, in weakness, seeing the scars, feeling the nail holes. Suffering is the precursor to resurrection. To recognize Christ's face in one's impending death will be no mean feat, and for some may be impossible. Nevertheless, when the whys have subsided and the listening and looking begin, then possibly—just possibly—one can get a glimpse of the mystery that is God.

The School of Suffering

A fifteen-year-old boy has too many beers, loses control of his motorcycle, crashes, and dies. In the aftermath his father, an alcoholic of twenty years, a has-been engineer frequently laid off from his job, an irascible and disagreeable character, cleans up his act. He gets off the bottle, dedicates himself anew to the church he had rejected as a teenager, takes a fresh interest in his wife and family, and becomes responsible again on the job. Out of a son's death comes a transformation of a father's life.

Now, it would be cruel and utterly absurd to say that God used the boy's death to teach the father a lesson. True, the father has turned his life around, but at what expense, the life of his child? Even such a remarkable turnabout can never justify such suffering and death. Suffering is simply inevitable. No one would ever wish for such a tragedy, but tragedies do occur. Suffering is a school where we can learn about ourselves, about our lives, and about God, and it can ultimately serve as a foundation for maturation.

Suffering, from a Christian perspective, has two components—the anguish itself, and the reflection or learning that occurs in response to the pain. Søren Kierkegaard writes,

"When a man suffers and is willing to learn from suffering then he constantly learns about himself and his relationship to God; this is the sign that he is being trained for eternity."[14]

Suffering is part of being human. The struggle to learn from suffering, to reflect on its depths, helps bring meaning to one's life. As undesirable as suffering is, it is a key to personality development and personal maturity. Certainly this has been a major theme in existential psychology, especially in the work of Victor Frankl.[15] Untold pastoral counseling sessions have begun with individuals describing some horror or tragedy, some physical or spiritual suffering, and almost in the same breath telling how it has changed their lives for the good.

The danger in suffering is that the disorganization and personality disintegration it brings may lead not to growth, but to despair and cynicism. There is always that potential. People who suffer do not invariably mature in the faith; some abandon it. Where suffering is concerned, the question is one not of bad versus good, all suffering is bad, but only of wasted suffering versus the reflected-upon anguish that brings depth and growth. The suffering itself and the evil that produces it is not what brings the good; if good there be, it is due to our active response that results in new learnings.

Ministers in particular have surely noted this. Some people we endeavor to help want only an adhesive bandage to cover the wound so they can go on as if little or nothing had happened. There are others, however, who desire not only to be relieved of the pain but also to learn from it. Learning from suffering is thus one hoped-for outcome in pastoral care. Suffering is a school that each Christian is called to attend. Again Kierkegaard writes of what we learn there:

Suffering itself is, from the human point of view, the first danger, but the second danger, which is still more terrible, is that we should not learn obedience. Suffering is a lesson full of danger; for, if we do not learn obedience—then it is as terrible as if the most efficacious of medicines had the wrong kind of effect! In such danger man needs help: he needs the help of God; else he learns not obedience. And if he does not learn obedience then he may learn the worst corruption—learn a cowardly hopelessness, learn a quenching of the spirit, learn to damp down whatever fire of nobility is in him, learn perverseness and despair.[16]

The academy of obedience does not teach us stoicism, a folding of the arms, a gritting of the teeth, and an emotional distancing from others; rather it teaches us an open-armed acceptance of our lot. Dorothee Soelle puts it this way:

The Christian idea of the acceptance of suffering means something more than and different from what is expressed in the words "put up with, tolerate, bear." With these words the object, the suffering itself, remains unchanged. It is borne—as a burden, suffered—as an injustice; it is tolerated, although intolerable; borne, although unbearable. "Put up with" and "tolerate" point to stoic tranquility rather than to Christian acceptance.[17]

Suffering and the Christian

In the apocalyptic books of Scripture the last stages of the world are characterized by terrible suffering: "tribulation" is the term applied to this aspect of apocalyptic chronology. The message is that the world, even the universe, is steadily degenerating from its original state at creation. Things are getting progressively worse. As we approach the end of time and enter this period of tribulation, the righteous will have to suffer, they above all. Why the righteous? Because in the last days the powers of evil gain the ascendancy, and the ruler of this world (as the devil is called in John 12:31; 14:30; 16:11) is determined to afflict the righteous in every way possible. The suffering of the righteous, then, far from being illogical or unexpected, is precisely what Christians must be prepared to face in the last times. Suffering will be the distinguishing mark of the Christian.

Although in scripture suffering is at times tied to one's sins, in the Beatitudes it is portrayed as a gift. Certainly what is meant here is not that we are to ignore suffering or pretend it does not exist, but simply that suffering that enhances communion with Christ is a source of joy, hence a gift. In Matthew 5 the Greek *makarios*, which is usually translated "blessed," may well mean "happy": "blessed" (or "happy") are those who suffer.

In his instructions to Christians (who happened to be slaves) the author of First Peter reminds them that they must suffer and endure pain, as God in Christ endured pain while suffering unjustly. The message again is that we must suffer. Suffering is a part of being Christian. God left us an example in Christ, who suffered for us, and we are to follow in his steps. (I Pet. 2:11-25).

For Paul ministry, to which all Christians are called, is not merely to speak the gospel, but also to live it. Since the heart of the gospel is the death and resurrection of Jesus, suffering is an integral part of the believer's ministry. We read much about the law of love; indeed it is one of the key concepts of the New Testament that in Christ the old bonds of the law are broken and the new law of love established. But what is often overlooked in twentieth-century Christianity is its companion, the law of suffering. As redeemed people of God we are charged to love others, but we also are called to suffer with Christ. Suffering is not only the lot of all humans; it is the particular calling of all Christians. To suffer is not good, for all suffering is indeed undesirable, but it is nevertheless right and proper. A hidden assumption that frequently lurks behind the theodicy question is the belief that somehow we Christians have a right *not* to suffer! On the contrary, suffering is to be expected, especially by Christians, since we are specifically called to follow the example of Christ. As Alastair Campbell points out:

Often the Christian churches put on the appearance of power and success, denying with their show of comfort and self-confidence, the bleeding and despised body of their Lord. But new life can come to suffering people when they find themselves in the company of those who, like Paul, are not ashamed to bear "the marks of Jesus branded on [their] body" (Gal. 6:17 NEB). Healing comes within a community of sufferers, because there, where weakness is freely acknowledged, the power of God's love can enter in.[18]

For Paul Tillich faith requires that we "accept suffering with courage, as an element of finitude, and affirm finitude in spite of the suffering that accompanies it."[19] Courage enables us to extract meaning out of suffering. Courage means facing existence and accepting suffering as a part of it. Our faith is that, in spite of the suffering, the way of the Spirit will be realized. Courage comes not out of strength but, strangely, out of weakness. It is the alternative to despair. As Dorothee Soelle puts it: "We don't have the choice of avoiding suffering and going around all these deaths. The only choice we have is between the absurd cross of meaninglessness and the cross of Christ, the death we accept apathetically as a natural end and the death we suffer as a passion."[20]

Pastoral Care and Theodicy

All extreme suffering evokes the experience of being forsaken by God. In the depth of suffering people see themselves as abandoned and forsaken by everyone. That which gave life its meaning has become empty and void: it turned out to be an error, an illusion that is shattered, a guilt that cannot be rectified, a void. The paths that lead to this experience of nothingness are diverse, but the experience of annihilation that occurs in unremitting suffering is the same.[21]

This comment of Dorothee Soelle reminds us of what we face in the ministry of pastoral care. How do we respond to suffering in a real-life situation, when a grieving person asks, "Why did God let this happen to me?" The question is hard, insistent, even paralyzing.

Even those ministers who are especially facile with words may find themselves hemming and hawing when confronted by the apparent conflict between God's goodness on the one hand and our seemingly needless human anguish on the other. There are no simple solutions to the conflict, but neither can we avoid facing it. It might be helpful at this point to suggest some technical considerations that can perhaps assist us in responding to questions of theodicy as a part of our pastoral care, and so translate the earlier theological discussion into the idiom of human relationships.

Ministers need to be prepared to face the issue of theodicy, for it will be encountered invariably and often in pastoral care and counseling situations. Therefore it is imperative that we consider our own personal struggles and losses, and that we read, think, and reflect on the theological issues they raise. In addition to such soul searching about our own suffering, and discussion with colleagues, I have found it helpful also to practice responding to specific cases, whether hypothetical or real, where the why question is raised. The case to be considered should be as realistic as possible. It is not easy, but it is beneficial, to act or try to act as the representative presence of the church, verbalizing one's own understanding of theodicy in concrete situations. Such preparation and practice may reduce somewhat the uneasiness we all feel in a crisis situation; not that ministers should have all the answers, but as interpreters and proclaimers of the faith we must be able to help others make sense out of this theological issue. Ministers who have reflected on the issue and discerned their own basis of hope may be less likely to become ensnared in the parishioner's confusion and loss and better enabled to offer the presence of the church, which is faith and hope, rather than simply compound the despair.

Assessing Why Questions

Why questions are bound to be asked in pastoral care situations. When they are asked, two immediate dangers arise.

In the first place there is the temptation for the carer to provide immediate answers without first establishing a solid relationship with the troubled persons and listening to their pain. Such answers may be spoken from a conservative theological stance, by restating some of the traditional responses to suffering; or they may be a liberal refinement or rebuttal of such traditional notions, by offering (for example) a process view of theodicy. In either event, to launch too quickly into a homily or lecture on suffering and theodicy, no matter how astute, is to ignore people's pain, while perhaps not even answering their *real* question.

At the other extreme there is the danger of simply reflecting or mirroring the question back to the questioner, the classical nondirective approach. The peril in such a response is that we may overlook the person's *real* questions, the ones that demand real answers. Frequently, though, the why question is itself a truly serious one. If the pastor nondirectively ignores it, that could ultimately affect the pastor-parishioner relationship in a negative way. At the very least, it might suggest to the parishioner that the minister is not comfortable with these serious theological issues.

What is important is not that ministers rush in prematurely with facile answers, or nondirectively evade the questions altogether, but that they bring to the situation their own prior reflection. Reflection upon our own suffering is part of the caring that listens to others' anguish. Our listening is the crucial thing, and it is not offered condescendingly by haves to the deprived have nots; it is rather a self-conscious participation in the common suffering of humanity.[22] As Campbell puts it:

The wounded healer heals, because he is able to convey, as much by his presence as by the words he uses, both an awareness and a transcendence of loss. . . . The wounded healer heals because he, to some degree at least, has entered the depth of his own experiences of loss and in those depths has found hope again.[23]

In chapter 2 on theological assessment it was noted that the why questions can often help ministers gain a clearer understanding of the parishioner's implicit and explicit theological assumptions. Discussion of a person's questions can disclose much about his or her views of God, sin, faith, and salvation.

When the why question is first raised, pastors must try to discern whether the individual truly wishes to discuss a theological issue, or whether the why question is rather a vehicle for expressing a sense of loss. Does it reflect a desire to understand what does not seem to be understandable, or is it rather a way to communicate one's pain? In my experience the questioner rarely intends either one or the other; rather a mixture of both is involved. As pastor it is my job, however, to discern which of the two is pressing for priority at any given time.

Many of the whys clients raise are actually *poetic questions.* They are a symbolic or metaphoric way of expressing depths of misery. Indeed, many parishioners may find it easier to ask, "Why did God do this?" than to say, "I have had an immense loss and am feeling utterly devastated by it." As a rule during shock or in the early phases of reacting to a recent or impending loss, most people use why questions primarily to voice their own anguish. This does not mean that the theodicy question is not also of concern—perhaps even their *real* concern—but only that in most cases emotional pain rather than curiosity is the driving force at the moment.

A helpful way to determine whether the why is poetic or literal is tentatively to assume that people are in fact expressing emotional hurt, and then operate first on that basis. The response to "How could God let this happen to me?" may be something like "John's death is really a great loss for you." This approach assumes that implicit within the why question being asked is a profound expression of grief, and that the pastor's task is to help the individual discern and express it. The individual who then replies with a verbal or implied "yes, *but*" is most likely a person genuinely searching for some sort of adequate answer to the why; indeed, some people seem emotionally unable to express grief until they have seriously and thoughtfully wrestled with the theodicy issue.

If, on the other hand, the individual latches onto the pastor's basically empathetic response, it is sensible to follow that track and facilitate the venting of feelings. In such cases, however, it is important that the minister not ignore or pass over the why question altogether, but consciously return to it at a later time. Although theodicy concerns may eventually diminish in emotive intensity after the person has had a chance to express sorrow—especially after some days, weeks, or months of becoming accustomed to the loss—the question usually will not go away by itself. In fact, as the intensity of the loss diminishes, the theodicy issue may come to the fore even more forcefully. The pastor who initiates a return to the question at a later session can provide an important opportunity for growth in the faith.

Embodying the Presence of the Church

A pastor who sits with people whose world has been turned upside down serves as a representative presence of the church in that situation. Where pastor and parishioner are gathered together at such times, there the church resides. The presence of one who believes, who has been redeemed by the Lamb, who rests in the gospel's hope, who is seen as a representative of God and the church on earth, can provide succor to the person who is troubled and hurting. The ministry of presence, including the listening ear and the dynamic power of the visible word can be for the person in suffering a door that opens onto new meaning in what had otherwise seemed like a barren and meaningless situation.

In the pastor's patient listening the person in pain can often sense this presence of the church. Allowing the expression of emotions felt about the tragedy can be a loving and helpful thing, for thinly veiled by the articulated whys may well be a consuming anger. As the church's representative, the pastor needs to expect and be prepared to meet a barrage of rage, all of which is basically directed against God.

I had just such an experience when I was still in college. Married and poor at that time, I routinely accepted almost any part-time job that could put food on the table. Near campus in the center of Minneapolis was a church that needed canvassers. I agreed to knock on doors in the neighborhood on their behalf, ask a few demographic questions, and inquire whether each resident had a church home. The job lasted only a week or two.

One beautiful spring afternoon, a tall and intimidating man with two days' growth of beard opened the door of his run-down duplex. He was wearing a heavy scowl and a dirty T-shirt. His very appearance stopped me cold for a moment. I quickly asked my questions, staring all the while at my clipboard. After barking a few terse one-word answers, he suddenly asked, "Are you a Christian?" I meekly responded that I was. He said, " Come in. I want to talk with you." We canvassers had been instructed that, after asking the survey questions, we should be willing to discuss faith or the church with anyone who wanted to do so. I loathed the idea of talking with this man but did not see a way out, so I followed him into his living room and sat on the couch.

After the door closed, the man began to storm for some fifteen or twenty minutes, which to me at the time seemed like an eternity. He raged on about the hypocrisy of Christians and screamed that God does not even exist, because if there were a God, God would not let innocent children be hurt and destroyed. Then the man told me how his own son had been run over by a car only six weeks earlier. He railed at me, "How could God allow my boy to be killed right in front of my own house?" Terrified by the sheer bulk of the man and the intensity of his anger, I stared feverishly at my lap, glancing up only occasionally to look for an escape route. There was none. I was trapped. Suddenly the man did something that was even more uncomfortable for a young college student to witness. He began to cry, in fact to sob, "You are the first person who has listened to me."

I could take no credit for listening. In fact I had heard little of what he said and would have slipped eagerly out into the street if I could have. But sitting there on the couch I learned something: The why questions and the angry epithets about Christian hypocrites were simply this man's way of telling how devastated he was by the death of his young son. He was still trying to make sense of the tragedy. He may have had real questions about the existence and goodness of God too, but for some six weeks now the primary issue was his grief and sorrow. Pastors who would embody the loving presence of the church at such a time need to be prepared to face anger and help in getting that anger expressed.

The Answers People Give

Over the years, while making pastoral care visits and especially hospital visits, I have sadly encountered many people whose well-meaning friends and acquaintances have responded to their why questions with theological answers that left them terribly upset and proved actually to be destructive: "This is God's punishment on you for your sins." "This is God's will; you have to accept it." "This has happened to bring you to the Lord." "God wanted your dear one with him in heaven." "If you hadn't skipped out on your wife, this wouldn't have happened." "If you had stayed home with your children where God wants you to be, they wouldn't have started taking drugs."

More recently I have also come across another whole class of answers—more psychological than religious—to theodicy issues: "You are responsible for your illness." "You are sick because of your destructive thoughts." "The cancer inside you is pent up anger; you've got to release it to get well." "You are what you eat; if only you had cut out salt and exercised more." Some people are so eager to give their answers that they scarcely wait for the questions to be asked. The results are often quite grim.

When I first began pastoral care work, I would have thought such pronouncements were rare, or occurred only in the more conservative denominations. Not so! Things such as this happen everywhere, regardless of the conservative or liberal orientation. Simplistic and damaging answers flow from well-meaning people at a time when their hearers are in considerable distress, vulnerable, and unable to talk back. I raise the issue here because if ministers care only for people's emotional pain and do not respond theologically to the issue of theodicy, parishioners will inevitably get their theological education elsewhere, and it may not be the kind we would have wished for them. In other words, if ministers will not respond, sooner or later, to the vital questions of theodicy, neighbors and friends are likely to do so, and not always in a helpful manner.

Another assumption I carry into pastoral care visits where

theodicy may be an issue is that the person has already received a medical explanation. In the loss that Karen and I experienced, it ran as follows: "The fetus was abnormal in some way and most likely would have been born with defects, or worse." Medical responses are usually offered by physicians, but they too can be voiced by other people, medical personnel as well as neighbors and friends. The variety of such medical explanations is endless: "You are young, you can have another." "He's out of pain now, and that's a blessing." "Better that she went quickly." "They would have suffered, or had brain damage, the rest of their lives." Sound medical explanations are often helpful; they can contribute to an improved understanding of what actually has happened or is happening. But such explanations also pose a problem: they do not deal adequately with theodicy. The why question has to do with meaning, and as such requires a theological answer.

It is important to remember that many people do not verbalize their why questions (I did not). But this does not mean they are not thinking about them—and hearing spurious advice about them. When counseling after a divorce, for example, we are careful to sense whether the individuals are experiencing guilt, even if they are verbalizing "everything is fine." Likewise, we need to be aware that in many pastoral care situations where simple faith in God's goodness clashes with the fact of personal suffering, people may not speak of it—they do not wish to "offend" the pastor—but their inner world is likely to be in desperate turmoil as they attempt to understand how a loving God can coexist with evil, can allow such suffering. Answers will mushroom all about them—answers that are superficial, possibly harmful, and surely fall short of the church's hope-filled message.

Crises and the Why Questions

Researchers in the area of human crises have pointed out that an acute crisis situation not only can affect an individual's emotional, physical, and intellectual life but also can turn one's values and sense of meaning upside down. In a previous book on crisis intervention I wrote:

Crises, besides causing upheaval in one's emotional, physical, and intellectual life, also cause a disturbance in one's values and sense of meaning in life. Every crisis has a religious potential. Crises raise basic questions. . . .

The minister or counselor who deals with the emotional, physical, or intellectual and ignores the spiritual and "meaning" aspects of a person's crisis is not responding to the whole person or using his or her unique training. During crisis a person may be especially receptive to Christian values and meaning if they are sensitively portrayed by the minister.

Paul Tillich defined pastoral care as [a] "helping encounter in the dimension of ultimate concern."* Upstanding members of a congregation may, during a crisis, question what they have previously affirmed in their Christian faith. In such a situation the minister must not be frightened, but remain emotionally "with" the person. His or her sensitivity and ministry of presence will help a person to weather these doubts.[24]

We have to assume that in crisis and loss situations profound issues of meaning and theodicy are being raised, whether or not they are articulated. The suffering experienced in such situations can be so immense that one of the first tasks of pastoral care is to help people put what they are going through into words. Such a "language of lament" can help them say the unsayable, to ask why, and thereby begin to move in the direction of needed acceptance and change.[25]

Talking About Theodicy

How do we then talk about theodicy, once we have discerned that the major pain is not primarily emotional but flows from a real desire to understand God and God's connection with tragedy? To speak of God and suffering

---

*From an address at the National Conference on Clinical Pastoral Education, Atlantic City, New Jersey, November, 1956.

requires great pastoral artistry and a careful listening for the word and to the word. Although it is not primarily a matter of technique, pastors may want to be aware of the following technical considerations when they talk to suffering people about theodicy.

Ministers must have done prior reflection; they must know what they themselves believe. We have said this before but it cannot be emphasized enough. Moreover, we are not to coerce others into adopting our religious views, but to enable them to achieve a better understanding of scripture and of their own faith. Surely it is a false dichotomy to suggest: *Either* I force my views on others *or* I say nothing to them at all. There is plenty of middle ground between these extreme authoritarian and *laissez-faire* positions. Ministers who would find and occupy that middle ground need only function in one of the standard pastoral roles—as prophet, proclaimer of the word, as enabler, or teacher. Parishioners need and want to know what the church has to say about theodicy; they probably will not have the privilege unless pastors care, proclaim, and educate to provide it.

An understanding of suffering requires not scientific questioning but faith and belief. Whatever methods of pastoral visitation and care are appropriate to the person's situation and religious tradition can also help that person to be grasped by the core of the gospel and gain insight into the whys. For if Kierkegaard is correct, that only out of faith can we understand suffering, then whatever nourishes faith also addresses the issue of theodicy. It may well be impossible for any minister to address the whys of someone perennially hostile to the church and to faith. For ultimately the issue of theodicy is resolved only within the gospel, not outside of it.

The why questions are real questions, bubbling up from the deepest center of one's being. They should not be turned into casual, abstract, ideological debate. Since each individual raises the questions in a slightly different way and out of a slightly different position in life, each needs to be addressed in a unique way. Stock answers will not suffice. Our response always must be contextually based—the result of a dialogue between the word and the specific situation. Ministers who have worked out their own views on theodicy will recognize the uniqueness of each person they encounter and tailor a response to that particular person. In my experience not all people are helped by the same set of metaphors about theodicy. Our task is to help clients search for those specific metaphors that hold truth for them.

Crisis intervention theorists have taught us that people who are in crisis, experiencing a loss or threat of loss, go through a period of heightened psychological accessibility. Their mistrust diminished, they undergo an increased openness toward learning from people who are there to help them. Thus a crisis can be a turning point in a person's emotional, intellectual, and spiritual well-being. Wilbur Morley's diagram of a crisis describes graphically this state of heightened psychological accessibility (see p. 170).

In the first diagram, a triangle represents the person who is *not* presently in crisis. Things are fairly stable. One of the three sides of the triangle is solidly planted somewhere on the continuum between mental health and the absence of mental health. A large portion of the person's psyche is fairly stable and can be relied on when the person is not in crisis, though a necessary consequence of such stability is that the person is less open to change. In normal life most people require this sizable degree of personality stability.

The second diagram shows a person who *is* in crisis, indicated by the triangle tipped up on end. Much less of the individual's personality is firmly planted on that line between mental health and the absence of mental health. The person is in a period of "upsetness" and vulnerability. The natural urge is to reestablish stability, so the person is more open to any influence—whether from inside or outside—that can aid in the resolution of the crisis. An optimal time for people to learn to deal with theodicy is when they raise the issue at a time of crisis. Since there is heightened psychological accessibility, the person is more open to new viewpoints than when the triangle is on its base. Frequently, after the most immediate and basic emotional needs are addressed, the issues of why can be discussed at a time when there is still this increased openness toward help from others.[26]

Morley's Diagram of Crisis

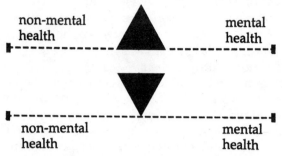

non-mental
health   mental
                                          health

non-mental   mental
health   health

When we talk with parishioners about why questions, it is best to begin by asking what *they* think, or have thought, rather than verbalizing our own views. We need to draw out their thinking, the answers they have heard from others and the answers that have made sense to them. As in any other area of counseling, it is best to explore first the feelings and thoughts of the client. We should listen carefully before responding. Sometimes it is helpful to ask direct questions: "Is that how you've always thought about it?" "What's troubling or confusing you now?" "What answers have other people suggested to you?" "What do you think of these answers?" "How has this episode shaken your faith?"

In our discussion of why questions, and especially as we try to help individuals find meaning in what at the moment seems to make no sense, we need to be careful not to imply that they *must* feel any particular way. When people are already feeling guilty for even raising a question about the goodness of God, if the pastoral carer baldly asserts that one ought to view suffering as a blessing they may end up feeling doubly guilty—not only for raising the question but also for viewing their suffering as bad. We should help people acknowledge their own feelings and bless them when they do. Frequently it is in the discussion of these feelings and related ideas, as they pertain to Scripture, that individuals begin to wrestle successfully with theodicy.

When speaking of our own understanding, our faith response to the why questions, it may be helpful to speak in image language. The worst possible response would be to start quoting a term paper on theodicy written back in seminary. For the faith-talk in which we are here engaged is not a theological discussion as expressed technically in the classroom. Our purpose is to speak simply, personally, and directly without jargon (though not condescendingly), while at the same time giving people the cognitive tools they need to help them begin making sense of their own plight. Many times this can be done through stories, parables, and Scripture (used not for proof-texting but to illustrate). The most helpful approach is to speak from your own experience of loss, your own struggle with the question of theodicy, sharing what has helped you, or others, in times of pain.

When we speak of the potential for growth and meaning that rises out of suffering, we should try to avoid the hard sell. Suffering is not a thing to be desired. It is a given that comes as a part of our finitude, not good but nonetheless inevitable—one that we can use for good or for ill.

A final thought. When we speak about suffering as a potential source of good, we cannot hope to wrap up the whole discussion by the end of the first session. At best we can only provide some initial material for continuing cogitation. Our task is not to convince vulnerable people who are in pain, but to help them shift their thinking just enough to look at their experience in a slightly different way, open to the possibilities of new interpretation.

When all is said and done, more Christians will probably get through the experience of evil and suffering with the help of a believer's quiet assurance of faith than with a scholar's discussion and critique of their theology. But both approaches provide ways in which God can speak the verbal and visible word—both the clear discussion of why questions and the loving presence of the church—through the minister. As we mature in the Christian faith, we arrive at ever deeper understandings of the relationship between human suffering and God's power and love. In the meantime, faced with evil, we may be able to do more than stammer, say a few words, and clam up. We may find it possible to be with them, to cry and feel helpless, but also to speak trustingly of the presence of a loving God who, though not the cause of their sorrow, can in its midst be their strength and release.

NOTES

1. Thomas C. Oden, *Pastoral Theology: Essentials of Ministry* (New York: Harper & Row, 1983), p. 223.

2. Ibid., for a short synopsis of the historical understandings of theodicy, pp. 223-48.

3. Langdon Gilkey, *Maker of Heaven and Earth* (New York: Doubleday & Co., 1959), p. 210.

4. I am indebted to my colleague Dr. David Gouwens for his help in elucidating the issues discussed here.

5. The Deuteronomic writer argued that God prospers the righteous and punishes the wicked. Therefore if evil occurs, it is God's punishment of one's wickedness. For example see Psalm 1.

6. Gilkey, *Maker of Heaven and Earth*, pp. 225-26.

7. Søren Kierkegaard, *The Gospel of Sufferings*, trans. A. S. Aldworth and W. S. Ferrie (London: James Clarke & Co., 1955), pp. 30-37.

8. Ibid., pp. 32-33.

9. Emil Brunner, *The Christian Doctrine of Creation and Redemption*, trans. Olive Wyon (Philadelphia: Westminster Press, 1952), p. 183.

10. Elie Wiesel, *Night*, trans. Stella Rodway, with a foreword by Francois Mauriac (New York: Farrar, Straus, & Giroux, 1960; Bantam Books, 1982), p. 32.

11. Ibid., pp. 61-62.

12. Ibid., pp. x-xi.

13. Gilkey, *Maker of Heaven and Earth*, p. 255.

14. Kierkegaard, *The Gospel of Sufferings*, p. 66.

15. Victor Frankl, *Man's Search for Meaning* (New York: Washington Square Press, 1963), pp. 105-16.

16. Kierkegaard, *The Gospel of Sufferings*, p. 55.

17. Dorothee Soelle, *Suffering*, trans. Everett R. Kalin (Philadelphia: Fortress Press, 1975), p. 103.

18. Alastair V. Campbell, *Rediscovering Pastoral Care* (London: Darton, Longman & Todd, 1981), p. 45.

19. Paul Tillich, *Systematic Theology*, vol. 2 (Chicago: University of Chicago Press, 1957), p. 70.

20. Soelle, *Suffering*, p. 157.

21. Ibid., p. 85.

22. Henri Nouwen, *The Wounded Healer* (New York: Doubleday & Co., 1979).

23. Campbell, *Rediscovering Pastoral Care*, pp. 42-43.

24. Howard W. Stone, *Crisis Counseling* (Philadelphia: Fortress Press, 1976), pp. 23-24.

25. Soelle, *Suffering*, p. 70.

26. Stone, *Crisis Counseling*, pp. 21-23.

Author Index

Subject Index